I AM
LIVING TRUTH
AN AWAKENING TO THE INTRODUCTION OF A LIFETIME

BOOK ONE: WHO ARE YOU?

I Am Living Truth
An Awakening to the Introduction of a Lifetime
Book One: Who Are You?
© Copyright 2021 by Katina Rodgers
for I Am The 1 Ministries Spirit School
ISBN: 979-8-9860082-3-3 (trade paperback)
ISBN: 979-8-9860082-0-2 (ebook)
www.iamthe1ministries.org

Editor: Katina Rodgers
Illustrator: Katina Rodgers
Audio Book Narrator: Katina Rodgers

Printed in the United States of America

DEDICATION

I dedicate this inspired works to the commissioner, the one and only true and living Abba God in my life. Without out You, faith, the gifts of prophecy and prophesying, this book wouldn't at all be possible. Lord, if I have said it once, I will say it again, I'm thankful to be chosen. I thank you for choosing me to be awakened to produce this great works on your behalf. My prayer is that the plans for this book, as it is written, does what You have purposed it to do. And because I know that it will, let this prayer manifest what this book came to do, in Jesus' name. I decree that the anointing God has placed on this book will transfer the desired need to every believer, to every non-believer, to anyone on the fence, to every reader, to anyone who touches, may come in contact with or passes by this book, in Jesus' mighty and precious name, Amen, Amen and Amen!
Luke 8:43-48; Mark 5:25-34

Additionally, I dedicate this book to you, the people of God. My hope is that you become official children of God. The God of Abraham, Isaac and Jacob has done this for you. Give Him a chance. If you tried everything else and it didn't work, you won't regret choosing to have the true and living God in your life. Not the misdirection of man, but the true direction of God. I pray for the gift of discernment to come upon you, to help guide you to the truth. My prayer is that you take this journey with God and allow Him to help you explore who you truly are, in Jesus' name, Amen.

ACKNOWLEDGEMENTS

Lord God, You are my Love, the Light of my life, the Path Finder to my journey home. I'll see You when I get there. And I want that hug when I do.

You are the One and only True and Living God, especially, to empower me, who is not much of a fan of reading, to become a best-selling author in a little over four months. Yes, I decree and declare this book will fulfill its purpose here on earth and become a number one best-selling book, in Jesus' name.

I say thank you to my wonderful husband, children, mom, aunt, uncle, sister, and a true friend who supported me in everything during this change. You all have been with me through the thick and thin of this all. I know it has been tiresome for you to hear what God was sharing with me. And as much as you all have listened and had no clue what was going on within me, by His grace, you all still managed to have a mustard seed of faith to support Him through me.

Especially my baby girl, she understood that I wasn't in my relationship with God just for myself. She understood that it's like joining the military. While everyone continues their walks in life, I was in the war room. I thank you for listening to me, for trusting in me, because if you trusted me, you had to trust Him. I love you even more for that. Besides Jesus, you all are my true ride and dies. You all embody the true charity of love God wants for us all.

Thank you.

CONTENTS

INTRODUCTION

I have three questions for you. If you don't have the answers to them now, that's okay; but if you have an idea or a concrete answer, please by all means write them down on the lines below. Although, I will only ask two things of you before you write them down:

1) please be honest, this book is for you, yes you, and it will be the beginning of a new journey for you, your life, and your life with God; and

2) please, use the lines below, as they will hold and bear witness to your remembrance of when this journey, you are about to take, began for you.

Okay, here it goes.....

Who are you? ___________________________________

____

____

Where are you from? ___________________________

____

____

Where are you going? ___________________________

____

____

Today's Date:___________________

You are probably thinking…boy, this is some introduction, and perhaps wondering where is this going? Yeah I get it, this introduction is not like any other typical introduction you will read in the beginning of a book. There are cases where some people or things need no introduction, and then, there are instances where an introduction is verily, verily, I say to you, truly necessary.

YOU ARE THE INTRODUCTION. You and your life are the introduction, and they both are very necessary for your promised lifetime. YOU and YOUR LIFE as you know it right now are quite the introduction needed for your awakening to the introduction of your lifetime.

What I mean by this is, imagine there are two of you. A You #1 and a You #2. You #1 is the current you, living as you are now; and You #2 is the you that you are promised to live.

The You #1 will acquire knowledge about itself that will ignite an awakening necessary for the introduction of itself to You #2.

The you and your life of You #1, as you are currently living right now are quite the introduction needed for your awakening. The position in the life of You #1 is exactly what is needed for the introduction to an awakening. The current status of You #1 will be introduced to an awakening. Now, the awakened You #1 will be introduced to the you and your life of You #2.

In summary, you, and your life, the who you are now, and your awakening to where you are now, which is the where are you from, will generate an introduction to the you, the you, you are promised to be and where you are promised to be going.

As you read on and engage yourself into a knowing, a knowing that will set you apart from the unknowing; you will find yourself in an awakening to an introduction to the truth of a lifetime. The truth which will release you into a freedom that's beyond the understandings of this world.

Here's the thing….

(**SECTION 1**: Please answer honestly. Check line a. or b. as it applies to you, then go to SECTION 2.)

______a. check here, if *you did not have the answers* or if *you at least have an idea* of the answers to the questions asked of you on the previous page. If you are unsure, then that is ok. The life as you know it now will only be the introduction to the life you are promised to LIVE. Life and the truth, right now, is not in you. **YOU ARE NOT LIVING IN THE TRUTH. Go to SECTION 2,** and check the answer that applies to you; or

______b. check here, if *you have concrete answers* to the questions asked of you on the previous page. Congratulations, you are living! Now it is time to learn whether you are LIVING in the truth. **Go to SECTION 2, and honestly answer** what foundation your concrete answers are supported by.

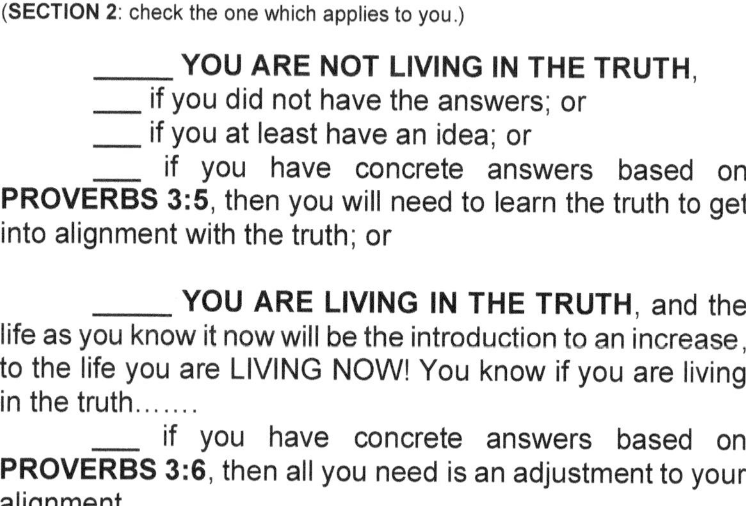

_____ YOU ARE NOT LIVING IN THE TRUTH,
___ if you did not have the answers; or
___ if you at least have an idea; or
___ if you have concrete answers based on **PROVERBS 3:5**, then you will need to learn the truth to get into alignment with the truth; or

_____ YOU ARE LIVING IN THE TRUTH, and the life as you know it now will be the introduction to an increase, to the life you are LIVING NOW! You know if you are living in the truth.......
___ if you have concrete answers based on **PROVERBS 3:6**, then all you need is an adjustment to your alignment.

Ok, so where are we going with all this? Now, by asking you, who are you, where are you from and where are you going, we are awakening your existence. Unfortunately, most of the population are walking in existence. For example, the existence of this book only proves existence. LIFE is what proves living. We awaken your existence when we pose these three questions to your thinking. Awakening your existence triggers your thirst for living. You will thirst for LIFE because you were not created for the bondage of existence, you were created for the freedom of living. When you accept the life in which you were created to live, you will prove living! You will prove LIVING TRUTH when you know who you are, and once you know who you are, then you will know where you are going.

YOU ARE LIVING TRUTH! The answer to who are you is YOU ARE LIVING TRUTH! Walking in existence is what separates you from living. And depending on how you answered the sections above, you are walking in a lie and you are simply unaligned. After reading this book series, you will be on your way into alignment. You will not only be LIVING TRUTH, but YOU WILL BE LIVING IN THE TRUTH.

(print your name here)

_______________________________, I introduce you to the
TRUTH as you will now know it to be:

The TRUTH that has been out there and will set you free from the bondage of existence;

The TRUTH that will either awaken you from a longtime lie; or will simply adjust your alignment in the truth;

The TRUTH that will free you to live free;

The TRUTH that will provide you with confident answers to know who you are, where you are from and where you are going; and

When you have the understanding of knowing, your knowing will set you apart from the unknowing. You will know who they are, and you will know who you are, where you are from and where you are going in The TRUTH that will prove you are LIVING TRUTH, LIVING IN THE TRUTH.

Let the truth be told from this day forward. You are going to experience an awakening of a lifetime, in Jesus' name, Amen!

"*For whosoever will save his life shall lose it: and whosoever will lose his life for my sake shall find it.*"(Matthew 16:25)

Chapter 1

Who Are You?

-you are living truth-

You are living truth. Why are you living truth? You are living truth because anything that couldn't be proven as true is otherwise false, right? Living Truth is something that is true proven by its existence. You reading this book right now proves you exist, so you are living truth; and your existence is proof this statement is true. You are living truth by the facts that:

___ you have breath;

___ you have life;

___ you have shape;

___ you have form;

___ you have a body;

___ you have a mind; and

___ you have a soul powered by your spirit, which requires the life source of the true and living Spirit, who is THE TRUTH.

Therefore, you are living truth of THE TRUTH. THE TRUTH is THE ONE AND ONLY TRUE AND LIVING GOD. "***And hereby we know that we are of the truth, and shall assure our hearts before him.***"**(1 John 3:19)** You see when we prove existence because of its existence, then we prove there is a life source of existence. THE TRUTH as we know Him is God, and anything created by God that either exists, or is living to talk about it, is Living Truth. And yes, this book is living truth too, as its existence was inspired by THE TRUTH to give you life. For "***All things were made by him; and without him was not any thing made that was made,***" this coming from **John 1:3**, simply means, when THE TRUTH created mankind, anything mankind creates is a creation of THE TRUTH. Mankind and the creations of mankind are products of THE TRUTH. When you take the life source of THE TRUTH from the creation, there is simply no creation. "***Then shall the dust return to the earth as it was: and the spirit shall return unto God who gave it.***"**(Ecclesiastes 12:7)**

For further understanding, here are a few Bible scriptures gathered in brief to summarize the making of mankind and all things created from THE TRUTH, as it was written by THE TRUTH.

"***In the beginning God created the heaven and the earth***."[(Gen1:1)]
"*And **God said, Let us make man in our image, after our likeness**: and let them have dominion over the fish of the sea, and over the fowl of the air, and over the cattle, and over all the earth, and over every creeping thing that creepeth upon the earth.*"[(Gen1:26)]
"*So **God created man** in his own image, the image of God created he him; male and female created he them.*"[(Gen1:27)]

"*And the LORD **God <u>formed</u> man** of the dust of the ground, and breathed into his nostrils the breath of life; and man became a living soul.*"[(Gen2:7)]

"*And **God blessed them, and** God **said** unto them, **Be fruitful**, and **multiply**, and **replenish the earth, and subdue it: and have dominion** over the fish of the sea, and over the fowl of the air, and **over every living thing that moveth upon the earth**.*"[(Gen1:28)]

"***For by him were all things created**, that are in heaven, and that are in earth, visible and invisible, whether they be thrones, or dominions, or principalities, or powers: **all things were created by him, and for him**.*"[(Col1:16)]

"***The earth is the LORD'S**, and **the fullness thereof; the world, and they that dwell therein**.*"[(Psa24:1)]

"***And he is before all things, and by him all things consist**.*"[(Col1:17)]

There you have it; you are living truth. You are the proof that your existence is part of a creation by something greater than yourself.

-you are living truth, explained-
Expand your knowledge! Go to the workbook (P.13) to answer the questions for each section.

I coined this expression "***you are living truth***" because it is a proven true statement that best describes the living of the living. If we break this expression up word by word, to define each word, then we begin to understand this statement as a whole.

you

The '**you**', we are referring to here is You. Hi, how are you? Yes, I am talking to you, but you don't have to answer that, if you don't want to. Did you catch that? We made a connection. We had a dialogue. There was an exchange. There was an exchange between you, the reader, and me, the **_author_**. Acknowledging you, then followed by the question, for instance in, 'hi, how are you' started your engagement with my voice. I hope you can see where I'm going with this because **God is Good!** We just acknowledged the existence of each other. You have proven me, and I have proven you. Yay, we exist!

are

The 'are' in this situation, defines. It is establishing an attachment to the existence otherwise known as a defining moment. You are the reader. You see, the word 'are' just defined who you are in this moment. In this moment, you are the reader. The word 'are' attached you to your existence in this moment, which is a reader. You are the reader because, **You Are Reading** this book. Aren't you? You don't have to answer that either, it has already been proven. Further, I will prove you as a reader of my book because of the exchange we had while you were reading it. And because, you will now know me as a person by the knowledge you will obtain about me while reading this book. You see, in your truth, you will learn about me as being the author of this book, since you either heard about the book or you just got your hands on a copy of this book, but you haven't started reading it yet. Let's be honest here, learning only touches the surface or shall I say, learning only touches the cover of this book; especially, if you haven't taken the time to read it. Now we can even say, in your truth, you will have gotten to know me as a person, by reading this entire book. Let's admit it, knowing a person is far better than just learning about a person.

Alright, now that I have proven you as the reader, how are you going to prove me, Katina, as the author? I am the author because, I Am talking to you. Aren't I? Nope, don't answer that either. By now, you have to be finding all this quite hilarious and at the same time, eye opening. We are still making an exchange here. We're having some good old dialogue, right? So, forget about the bio and the photo if there is one. I don't really like being the subject of anything, let alone a photo, but I do love photography. There, you know a little bit more about me and you will find out more. How will you know me if you haven't met me personally? You will learn to discern. Right now, your proof that I am the author of this book is the control that I have in the writing. I have the controls over what is written and what you are reading. You are reading what I want you to read right now, because this is what you are reading. How are you getting to know me? What are you discerning? You are probably wondering, is she a funny person? Well, I can be. If my writing hasn't hinted to you by now, that I can be humorous, then in the least my writing should give my identity an image, the image that tells you all about my likeness. What is this saying? This is saying, even though you can't see me as you are reading this, you can hear my voice through my writing, right? I mean, you might be reading this in your voice, but my words are my voice. I have the controls remember. You just changed the sound of my voice by reading the voiceover. This is so hilarious. I am being so spiritually lifted right now; you have no idea.

HOLY SPIRIT HAVE YOUR WAY! HOLY SPIRIT HAVE YOUR WAY! Father, I pray that everyone who is reading this book with you right now is anointed by your presence, in Jesus' name, Amen.

As you continue reading this book you are getting to know me more and more. You know my sound, you know my voice, you know my existence. This book proves my existence. Everything you are reading in this text will help you to understand my personality; and anything personal I share with you, allows you to know me personally.

I'm hearing pen pal. Wow, what a revelation! **God is Good!** God is reminding me of a childhood memory of when I was paired with my first pen pal and only best friend. Besides having siblings and being around my neighborhood friends, I didn't have any other relationships outside of my block. I was about to start a new relationship, when I received my first letter ever from someone I didn't know, nor have I ever seen before. This experience was exciting and scary all at the same time. I had a real imaginary friend who was actually a real person. And what I mean by imaginary, in my mind at the time was invisible. After all, the only clue I had of her existence was in that first letter. Oh, I had to write back!

Honestly, the funny thing is, up until now, I kid you not, along with this revelation, I just realized the meaning of what a pen pal is. I always understood a pen pal as being friends who wrote each other, but the real revelation of this all was putting the pens to the paper that made us pals. Even though at first write, we didn't know each other or haven't seen each other, we knew each other existed and with each letter we wrote, we couldn't wait to write each other back. I didn't know when the next time I was going to hear back from her. We didn't have each other's phone number, so I couldn't even call her. I want to say by the third time we wrote each other, we had gotten to know each other well enough to prove a true existence. We were both readers and we were both authors. **God is Good!**

I know where God is going with all this. Do you know where He is going with all this? Have you read the Bible? That book is God's book, by the way. **HE IS THE AUTHOR of the KING JAMES VERSION**, which in a span of 1,500 years has 40 documented authors who were all inspired by the Holy Spirit. Ironically, I recently inquired of the Lord about why many people defer to, or make such a big deal about other versions of the Bible and just like that, He referred to those other books as being written by authors of confusion, "***For God is not the author of confusion, but of peace, as in all churches of the saints.***"**(1 Corinthians 14:33)** He goes on to share, many religions were formed from the books of these authors of confusion. Not too long after that, I heard the word 'catfish'. Right away my thoughts immediately met this strong impression in my spirit that God's identity is being stolen. The enemy, Satan the Devil, yeah that one, who has come to steal, kill, and destroy, has been deceiving mankind for years. All it took was for the devil to influence mankind to lean on its own understanding, for citing their own interpretation of God's Word and creating this image of who they thought or wanted God to be, otherwise also known as ***idolatry***, and the rest is history. The core values of God's identity were stolen, then mankind adds a little bit of this and leaves out a little bit of that. Voila!

There you have it, identity theft with a whole lot of confusion, and peace is nowhere to be found, except in the King James Version of the Holy Bible. Let's be real, mankind is being 'catfished' and we don't even realize it. Look at how smart mankind is, we can watch the tele-a-vision show, *"Catfish"*, of someone being deceived, but fail to realize, we the people as a whole have been misled for centuries. Of all the scholars out here, you mean to tell me no one, including me, could figure this out, just plain foolishness. We truly can't do anything on our own. God's divine revelation inspired my spirit with this eye-opener; and I'm pretty sure He has a lot to say to you too, if you will just let Him.

I normally don't like a lot of attention. I say this to say, the only reason why I stressed that I am the author of this Holy Spirit inspired book, is to drive the point home of proving existence, and while I'm at it, you wouldn't dare allow anyone steal your published works, let alone your identity; and let them get away with it. Well God isn't either, and He will get the Glory for it. Even though we don't naturally see God, it doesn't mean He doesn't exist; and just because we don't naturally hear Him, it doesn't mean He has no voice. And just because there are things that happen that you don't like or can't begin to understand, that doesn't mean it is His fault. The more we read the Word of God, the more we'll begin to understand once we get to know Him better.

*"**But as it is written, Eye hath not seen, nor ear heard, neither have entered into the heart of man, the things which God hath prepared for them that love him.**"*
(1 Corinthians 2:9)

In the end, you and I together define the word 'are'. All I would have to say is, 'you are the reader'; and all you would have to say is, 'you are the author'. You and I proved 'you are the reader' of this book, by establishing an attachment, attaching you to who you were in that defining moment of your life. All we had to do is prove existence, and when we prove existence, we prove life. Asking questions such as, where were you, what were you doing and what were you wearing while you were reading this book are just some questions supporting the evidence of your already proven existence. And if we are so wise, in our discernment to ask the appropriate questions, we are sure to get the right answers we are looking for. At the end of the day, all we must do is prove existence. When we prove existence, we prove life. When we prove life, we prove power. Whose power? That right there, is an appropriate question requiring the gift of discernment, for getting the right answer, to start living your life. As a result, as reader and author, we proved existence in each other's absence, we did it without sight of each other, we did it without the audible sound of each other and we most certainly did it without the touch of each other. We proved you are, we are, and God is. The proof is in the existence.

Mankind > Existence > Live > Power...Whose Power?

"I exist to live, and I live to eternally exist."
-Katina Rodgers-

living

     The '**living**' in the second half of this expression, '**you are living**', clearly tells you, '**you are living**'. Truthfully, this is who you are from an in-depth perspective when we are talking about existence. You are a living organism of matter. What's the matter? The kind of matter that makes up man's kind. In this case, mankind and all the kinds of man. These and all kinds stem from man, woman and children of all nationalities and races. Man's kind is what separates itself from all the other earthly kinds. The other earthly kinds that the Bible references are the fish of the sea, fowls of the air, beasts and creeping things that roam the Earth. The difference in man's kind from other Earth kinds is mankind's image, after God's likeness to subdue the Earth, and to have dominion, in god-like superiority over all of the other earthly kinds.

truth

     Lastly the '**truth**' of all the words will be the word that sets you free. "***And ye shall know the truth, and the truth shall make you free.***"(**John 8:32**) '**Truth**', the last word in the expression '**You Are Living Truth**' is strong. This word is the final word of a true statement that is the truth. The word '**truth**' is the foundational support of this statement, which confirms who you are, like a last name per se. When you know your last name, you know your family, you know who you are, and you know where you are from. And when we put this word '**truth**' in this context, it is true and substantiated by the TRUTH. Additionally, this word also tells you not only who you are, but whose you are. You are living truth is a true fact. Your existence or quality of living is proof of this statement. When you are made aware of this statement, you can do one of two things, you can continue to exist as you are or you can begin to live, and then begin to talk about it. You truly become living proof of living truth when you start living, and then begin to tell others about it. You start living in the truth that you were meant to live. Your unawareness and unacceptance of this term only proves your existence. You see we all are living truth; it is our acceptance of the TRUTH that makes the difference in claiming this term for our life as ours or not. Are you ready to accept your truth? Are you ready to live? Are you ready to start living in your truth?

There you have it, it's true! **You. Are. Living. Truth.** Each word in this expression was broken down and defined to put you back together again. You Are Living Truth, is a true statement because you are living proof of existence. You. Yeah, You. You Are You. You Are You because You Are. You Are the Truth. You Are the Truth because the Truth is within You. When you ***abide*** in the truth, the truth will abide in you. You start an agreement of alignment, which launches you both to abide within each other. The moment you abide in the truth, a supernatural birthing experience occurs, allowing for you to awaken to your promised living. Start Living In Your Truth. Don't just exist, exist to live, and you will live to eternally exist.

*"**Behold, thou desirest truth in the inward parts: and in the hidden part thou shalt make me to know wisdom.**"* **(Psalm 51:6)**

"Live, Don't Cheat Life."
-Katina Rodgers-

-you are created as spirit, formed a man-

Expand your knowledge! Go to the workbook (P.33) to answer the questions for each section.

created as spirit

To make a pretty long story short, ***you are living truth created as spirit, but formed a man***. You were created as spirit first, but then, formed a man kind, second. The scripture tells us in **Genesis 1:26**, God the Father, of the God Head communes with God, the Word (Son), of the God Head, and God, the Holy Spirit, of the God Head, and He says, "**Let us make man in our image, after our likeness.**" And "*So **God created man** in his own image, the image of God created he him; male and female created he them.*" So, God in all of His Glory and Power creates a spirit form, in His image and after His likeness. I used this example, when giving my family a visual during this demonstration. **WARNING: ANY VISUALS MADE DURING THIS DEMONSTRATION ARE NOT AND WILL NOT BECOME IDOLS. THEY WERE USED AS VISUALS FOR THIS DEMONSTRATION ONLY!** I took a cotton ball and stretched it out to give it the appearance of a larger piece of matter. Then, I took a small piece of cotton from the larger stretched piece of cotton, giving the smaller piece of cotton, the same qualities God gave to man's kind. Hence, calling the smaller piece of cotton, mankind. This smaller piece of cotton, we call mankind is God's creation, in His image, after His likeness. Now that's some creation! And you my friend, just met the identity of your true creation. Your first birth. Your spiritual birth. Who are you? You are living truth, created as spirit. ***HAPPY BIRTHDAY!***

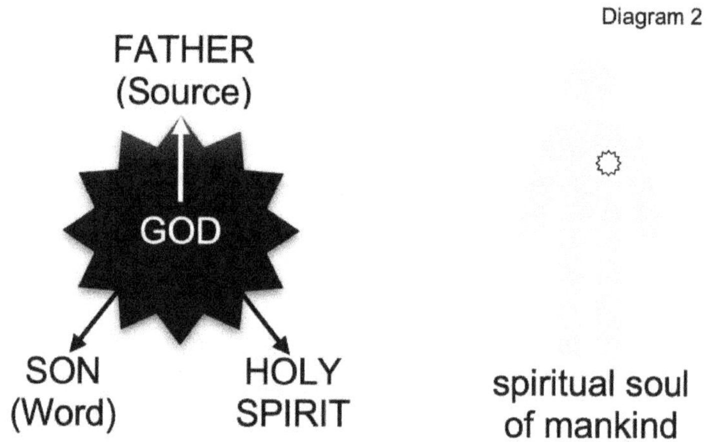

I'm going to go ahead and go there, so that I can get this out of the way. Let's address the elephant in the room. Woo-hoo, Holy Spirit have your way! I don't know if this is a spoiler alert to whether this is a part of God's image or after His likeness, but the Word as God indeed has a Word for the Body of Christ. God, the Father; God, the Word (Son); and God, the Holy Spirit, together as ***one body***, in its glory and power, created man's kind right along with all other kinds. We should learn from this. God in His total self, says, 'let us'; and the Word and the Holy Spirit say, 'yeah, let's do this!' The Word says, I'll speak it into the atmosphere, and the Holy Spirit says, okay, by my power, I'll give life to its existence. NOW WOULD YOU LOOK AT THAT! Look at how well they work together! Look at what God is showing us. He is showing us how **we should work together** *in His image* and *after His likeness*, **operating in unison under our respective functions**. Just look at that! Look at that nugget right there! ***One Body***, ***Three Functions***, as **_The Body of God_**, getting the work done!

I'm seriously shaking my head. We need to use these nuggets supernaturally being given to us here. We have The Body of God showing us how we should operate in each of His respective functions as the Body of Christ. I never looked at this analogy in this way. And when it comes to God's image, after His likeness, I wonder if anyone else has. If not, you know this is nothing but God, showing up and showing out in the most needed time of our lives. With that said, it's about time you find out who you are in the Body of Christ. You. Yes you. The one of God's many children. What is your function in the Body of Christ? You know who you are. You know, you are living truth. You know, you are God's creation. And you know, you are created as spirit. You know you are a spiritual being bearing the spiritual qualities of God. Therefore, what spiritual gifts has God impressed upon you during your spiritual birth and during your maturity? If you don't know or are unfamiliar with where to look, 1 Corinthians 12, is a good place start.

Summing this all up, words can't even begin to express the miraculous nature of beings we are. With knowing that we are created in God's image, after His likeness, we are spirit as God is spirit. Then the next question to ask is, what is the image of God's spirit and what image should be in the spirit of man?

formed a man
"***And the LORD <u>God formed man</u> of the dust of the ground, and breathed into his nostrils the breath of life; and man became a living soul.***"**(Genesis 2:7)**

The Body of God, in all His greatness, had this creation He called mankind. Mankind was created as spirit in God's image, after His likeness. Remember that small piece of cotton taken from the bigger piece of cotton demonstration I told you about earlier? Well, that example was to help us draw the conclusion that that small piece of cotton was only the ***<u>blueprint</u>*** for what God had in mind. When you think about it, the blueprint is the final set of plans for a creative design just before it becomes complete in all of its dimension and form. There is something crucial we need to realize here; God became a Father before He was an architect or is it the other way around? He is Elohim.

Did you know that God wanted children because He wanted a family?

In **Genesis 1:26**, when God says, "***Let us make man in our image, after our likeness***," we could say God is talking to Himself, and when we are talking to God, we could say, we are talking to ourselves too, right? I pray that you catch the spiritual observation in that. **God is Good!** Ok, God is talking. Who is God talking to? God the Father, of the God Head, our Creator, is talking to the Word and Power deities of Himself, as a whole, we call The Body of God. I'll explain as I'm envisioning this. God suggests the idea of making mankind's creation while in communion with the Word and the Holy Spirit. Knowing the Word of God, the plans for mankind's inspired design were already written for God's purpose. If we know anything about our Heavenly Father, we should know He has a store house full of books containing preexisting ideas, just waiting for their suggested time of creation. Then the Word goes to retrieve what was written, readying Himself to speak it into the atmosphere for the manifestation of life existence by God's power. God's visions are already written and made plain. Time is the only thing that separates those blueprints from their formal creation. And so are the rest of the visions He has purposed for each and every one of us. That's why God says to write the vision and make it plain, because God's desires are already imprinted and impressed upon us. We just have to want it and go after it. That's the alignment, if it's purposed and already written for you, you just have to come into alignment with God to manifest it. If the creation is already there, you just have to find it. And so, if God is giving it to you while He is communing with you, He wants you to write the vision and make it plain. God will provide everything for you to get it done, all you have to do is get it done. And you may ask, what's in it for God, um, He just wants the glory for it. Like any proud Father wanting to make His children happy. God is a miraculous God and doing things for us miraculously is His specialty. God's pleasure is to please us, and our pleasure should be to glorify Him by giving Him the best testimony ever. Whatever makes us happy makes Him happy. That's the glory, the joy or to put it plainly, this is what feeds God. Glory, happiness, and pleasing us is God's specialty and spiritual food. That's why we feel so good when we see the benefits of our good deeds. What spiritually feeds us in that way is the same thing that feeds our Father.

So, as it is written, in its perfect timing, a thing will be manifested for a purpose bigger than you could imagine, and that's **_His purpose_**. So, there will be a time when you find you are talking to yourself, but you are actually talking to God Spirit-to-spirit, the same way He communes with the Word and the Holy Spirit of Himself. Remember that spiritual observation I mentioned awhile back, well our relational God is the same way in Himself that He is within us, that voice in our mind.

As we are written for God's purpose, we are one in the same. God, our Creator has creations for our purpose that's for His purpose. He's full of visual ideas always creating. Up until now The Body of God is working and never stops working. Jesus says so himself in **John 5:17**, so why stop at the blueprint? The only thing to do now was to take this marvelous idea and manifest its being into material existence. The Body of God doesn't miss a beat to cohesively work in unison, The Word of God is spoken for the manifestation of a thing; and the Holy Spirit of God brings forth its Power for the life of a thing. "***And the LORD God formed man of the dust of the ground, and breathed into his nostrils the breath of life; and man became a living soul.***"**(Genesis 2:7)** Elohim our Creator, the Father and Architect of mankind "***formed man of the dust of the ground,***" making its kind an earthen vessel, what we call the body and otherwise known as the flesh, to encapsulate the spirit, soul, mind, conscience and other bodily functions for the living and reproduction of man, "***and breathed into his nostrils the breath of life; and man became a living soul.***" No matter how many times we reread these words of God regarding the creation of man, we seem to lose the significant understanding that man is created in God's image, after His likeness encased in a body. The only other exceptional difference to God's creation of man was mankind's level of power and godliness. Prior to sin, man was assigned a form of godliness along with having the flexibility to travel throughout the heavens, while under God's command to have dominion and subdue rulership over the Earth. In Diagram 1, the human figures are purposely located outside of the Earth for this reason.

And now here in Diagram 3, we have an illustration of what we otherwise couldn't see person-to-person, and what I'm sure Moses would have provided as a visual for **Genesis 1:27**, to illustrate exactly what we can't understand when God incorporated himself into humankind as a spiritual masterpiece, of an immortal soul, an extraordinary mind and a moral conscience, in His image, after His likeness, and otherwise known as the most inward parts of every man kind. "***Even the Spirit of truth; whom the world cannot receive, because it seeth him not, neither knoweth him: but ye know him; for he dwelleth with you, and shall be in you.***"**(John 14:17)** Plain and simple, the most inward parts of mankind consists of our Heavenly Father's DNA. Then, further down in **Genesis 2:7**, the outer layer of mankind, known as the flesh, was formed from the dust of the ground, the strongest organ of the human body holding everything in its place, supported by the bones to structurally give human bodies the stability it needs. Thus, God's creation of the Earth was not only limited for the nature and nurture of mankind, but for the fashioning of mankind. Therefore, mankind's body of flesh and bones is made up of Mother Earth's DNA providing identification temples for every individual being of God. "***What? Know ye not that your body is the temple of the Holy Ghost which is in you, which ye have of God, and ye are not your own? For ye are bought with a price: therefore glorify God in your body, and in your spirit, which are God's.***"**(1 Corinthians 6:19-20)** "***For the invisible things of him from the creation of the world are clearly seen, being understood by the things that are made, even his eternal power and Godhead; so that they are without excuse.***"**(Romans 1:20)** With the Holy Spirit's guiding of this revelation and its supporting biblical scriptures, there are no excuses necessary to come up with any other theological interpretations of what we think the anatomy of mankind is to be. Yes, He did make the mind to be extraordinary, but let's not use it to lean on our own understanding. "***Trust in the Lord with all thine heart; and lean not unto thine own understanding.***"**(Proverbs 3:5)** I say we continue to partner with Him, who made all things, for more revelations, because that's the only way we can add to what was just explained here.

"***And we know that all things work together for good to them that love God, to them who are the called according to his purpose.***"**(Romans 8:28)**

Think about this for a minute, every living soul of man is a spiritual masterpiece of God, with its own temple identification making every human being an internal clone of Himself. What makes humankind a master piece of the True and Living God, is that everyone who has its own temple identification, we call a body made of flesh and bones, is a singular spiritual cell of living soul with its own mind and conscience. You know that saying God is everywhere. WELL, HE IS. He, Himself as Spirit is literally everywhere; and He is spiritually and naturally Himself in everything He has made everywhere. "***All things were made by him; and without him was not any thing made that was made.***"**(John 1:3)**

Let's do a quick recap for further understanding:

- in **Genesis 1:27**, God first created a clone of Himself in His image, after His likeness, He then calls the said clone of Himself, mankind. Mankind is a spiritual life form bearing the fruits of God's Spirit, otherwise known as having God's DNA, and man's source of spiritual life. We call man's created life form, his spirit life form or spiritual life form.
- And then, in **Genesis 2:7**, God formed a temple for His cloned self, from the soil of the Earth's ground, He then calls the said temple for Himself, flesh. Additionally, mankind is a natural life form having a regenerative body of flesh and bones from Earth's nature, otherwise known as having the Earth's DNA, and man's source of natural life. We call man's formed life form, his body life form or natural life form.

"Howbeit the most High dwelleth not in temples made with hands; as saith the prophet"(Acts 7:48)

"God that made the world and all things therein, seeing that he is Lord of heaven and earth, dwelleth not in temples made with hands."(Acts 17:24)

To help you better understand the above scriptures, God is Holy and will only dwell in Holiness. God will only dwell in the Holiness made by His hands, thus, God will only dwell in Holiness fit for a King. And so, God made for Himself a natural life form (body), to house His spiritual life form (spirit), which was intended to lead and guide the souls, mind, and conscience of all of mankind. God is. God is mankind's spiritual guide, so let's put the temple in cruise control and let the internal navigator lead.

Ok, the spiritual (internal) and natural (external) life forms of mankind consist of these five parts: body, spirit, soul, mind, and conscience. In addition, both spirit and body life forms have the use of five capable living senses for seeing, hearing, smelling, tasting, and touching. And so, both life forms of mankind's spirit and body are accessible to the soul, mind, conscience, seeing, hearing, smelling, tasting, and touching, which all can cohesively work together or independently on their own. Phew, I hope y'all got this. **HOLY SPIRIT, HAVE YOUR WAY!** Our senses help us to enjoy life, make decisions and get around, so for the purposes of where we are going next, we're going to focus on choice; but first we will have to go deeper in the meanings of spirit, body, soul, mind, and conscience to understand what it means when God allows choice as He guides our lives.

Since we are spiritual creatures of God, we will start with who we truly are first.

1. The spirit man of mankind is the life source of who we are. For it was from the Spirit of God by whom we were given the breath of life when *"the Lord God formed man of the dust of the ground, and breathed into his nostrils the breath of life; and man became a living soul."*(Genesis 2:7) God

breathed the breath of life for mankind's eternal and natural life forms. And not only does the Spirit of God give life, but from the same are His characteristics, the pure essence of "***the fruit of the Spirit is love, joy, peace, longsuffering, gentleness, goodness, faith, meekness and temperance: against such there is no law.***"**(Galatians 5:22-23)** See more on the fruit of the Spirit later in this chapter, you are created after His likeness. And so, we learn, the Spirit of God is our source of life and the essence of our life, which entitlement rightfully gives us access to the spirit realms. We must be careful when entering these realms, which is why we should know that our walk with God is sound before doing so. Reflect on the spiritual warfare chart in the workbook to comprehend this understanding.

2. Although the soul of mankind is of its own, it works hand-in-hand with our spirit man. The soul is one of the driving forces of man's ***emotions***: happy, sad, love, hate, passion, wrath, doubt, joy, fear, and excitement, etc. Often times the soul of a man can swing from mood to mood if the allowed motions are not in check. And usually finding the root is the best place to check where the moving expression came from, if unhealthy emotions become problems.

3. The body of a man, at best when first described in Genesis 2:7, is its form. You may want to describe it as a house, home, zoot suit, space suit, or a body of flesh and bones. The body or the flesh of man

houses everything. Each one separate and apart from one another as its own identification. The body, a living flesh, is the thing that separates the identities, one from another. The body is man's identification, but the heart is God's. Whatever the case, know that man's body is a miraculous natural wonder of God, it is His temple that He allows you to abide.

4. Besides, man's thoughts, what more can we say about the mind? How about the fact, it is also the place where free will comes from. Actually, it's the thought process, which helps with the choices that are made when free will is exercised. Again, these parts are separate entities, but they become powerful forces when effectively working together. Just like the spirit and soul, the mind and conscience are closely knit together when having to make the best decisions.

5. A man's conscience is the keeper of his moral compass. Will the compass meter turn left, or right, up, or down, for legal, or illegal, moral, or immoral, good, or evil, in right, or wrong situations. There is one thing for sure, man's moral compass does work, it's whether man decides to listen to it or not, that's the key. And the cohesive works of an effective mind, soul and spirit are contributing factors when achieving the best results.

The Body of God demonstrates for man throughout the Bible how effectively well they work together; but for some reason, mankind still manages not to get it right. And for the same reason, Jesus had to come and tell the Chosen and many others to 'follow me'. God has always been first to lead by setting the example. **He even went as far as demonstrating this with Abraham all while showing him what it was going to take.** And of course, through experience mankind is always the first to offend God. All the while, He remains being the bigger person, in hopes that we would eventually get it right. If we'd only love Him first, as He commands us, we wouldn't offend God and we'd be free from sin. Like God, we would have to be the first, the first to forgive seventy times seven. Unfortunately, because of man's natural ways, our hyper emotional souls boil the skin so fast, that anything God has taught us goes right out of the window. Everything the mind, soul and body tries to convince the conscience into believing against the spirit, is now right, when it is dead wrong. God gave us a brain with a mind to think, so that we would use it for others first, and not just ourselves. We're in a day and age of another breaking point. God is setting it off, to give us another chance. **Are You Ready? Get Set. RESET!**

We're about to learn a lesson in the importance of identifying the first responder before we respond. It is critical to understand who is being offended, so that they lead the response to the offense. **IT'S TIME FOR SOME EXERCISE!** HEAD TOWARD THIS SECTION (P.53) OF THE WORKBOOK.

EXERCISE 1: WE ARE GOING TO TEST OUR FIRST RESPONDER MECHANISMS BY IDENTIFYING WHO IS USUALLY FIRST TO RESPOND, WHO SHOULD RESPOND, WHOSE HELP SHOULD THEY GET WITH THE RESPONSE AND HOW SHOULD THEY RESPOND. THIS IS AN AREA WHICH REQUIRES MUCH NEEDED ATTENTION. MAKING A CHANGE IN WHO IS THE FIRST TO RESPOND ONLY REQUIRES A RENEWING OF THE MIND WHEN LEARNING HOW TO RESPOND.

God's purpose for the essence of every man is to have the fruit of the Spirit lead him as a tour guide through life, and everything else beyond that is man's character. The character of every individual is what makes us all uniquely different. This silhouette of our spiritual lifeform in totality is otherwise identified as the quality of a man's heart; and because of the free will given to him by God, the quality of man's heart is from where God will judge. God's image of fruitful godliness should reside in the quality of every man's heart, but because of sin, there was a separation leaving many to disconnect completely from God or malfunction in general. In the end, God judges a man's heart through the free will given to him. Now that you have a better understanding of this information, what will the heart of your free will choose?

To get a better understanding of God's heart on the matter, the creation of mankind was birthed from the longing idea of a loving God to have someone and something else exist other than Himself, like Himself. God wanted to have children; God wanted to have us. Yes, God created Angels, but He created the Angels for us not like us, **Psalm 91:11**, and so mankind's creation became a desired manifestation from the Spirit of God to be the spirit of man. God is giving me this thought, so I'm going to include it. We see couples longing for a child every day, so there. Mankind was intended to live in God's image, after His likeness of Spiritual Godliness. And like every natural parent, we want our children to look like us, be like us and possess qualities just like us.

Look at what the Lord is showing me through this example, when God created Adam, He created Adam to be exactly like Himself. Adam is the offspring of God, who is an exact replica of His Father with the same abilities of His Father. God is the one who creates, He's the one who determines. As the godhead of mankind, God created Adam in this same manner. Adam is head of household, in relations with Eve, Adam is the one who creates, because without Adam nothing would be made and the same goes for Eve too, but from this perspective, Adam's semen is what determines the sex of the offspring. God positioned Adam in the same view of Himself. The Earth, on the other hand, also a creation of God, is the Mother of all living. In this identical capacity, Eve was created the same, "***And Adam called his wife Eve; because she was the mother of all living.***"(Genesis 3:20) God had given Adam and Eve the command to be fruitful and multiply. Like God, Adam is the creator, and during the relational time necessary, he and Eve creates; and Eve, the mother of all living, is required for a period of time to give the creation its form; and she being likened to our Mother Earth, gives birth to all of mankind.

"And as we have borne the image of the earthy, we shall also bear the image of the heavenly." (1 Corinthians 15:49)

We're about to express from the lesson learned on God's heart of the matter. **IT'S TIME FOR SOME EXERCISE!**

EXERCISE 2: NOW WITH KNOWING GOD'S HEART ABOUT HAVING CHILDREN AND HOW HE WOULD HAVE HAD CHILDREN, IF HE WERE A MAN, IN WHICH TECNICALLY HE IS OF HIS OWN, AND THROUGH EACH AND EVERY ONE OF US. THIS IS WHY HE SAYS TO BE FRUITFUL AND MULTIPLY. HE DESIRES IT! NOW KNOWING THAT GOD FEELS THIS WAY, WRITE A LETTER OF UNDERSTANDING TO GOD. A LETTER OF COMPASSION, FROM YOUR HEART TO HIS HEART ON WHAT YOU LEARNED, KNOW, AND UNDERSTAND ABOUT HIS HEART'S DESIRES WHEN IT INVOLVES HAVING A FAMILY AND CHILDREN. WRITE ABOUT WHAT YOU WILL DO BETTER. WRITE WITH RESPECT TO YOUR APPRECIATION FOR LIFE. WRITE ABOUT WHAT YOU WILL DO TO SHARE THIS INFORMATION TO FATHERS, TO MOTHERS, TO CHILDREN TO EVERYONE, ABOUT KNOWING GOD'S HEART ON THIS MATTER.

HEAD TOWARD THIS SECTION (P.59) OF THE WORKBOOK AND BEGIN TO WRITE! IF YOU DON'T HAVE THE WORKBOOK, GET SOME SHEETS OF PAPER, PAUSE HERE AND START WRITING NOW!

Whether we like it or not, there are two life forms to man's DNA. There is the spirit man, which is from God, our Father's side, and what we'll identify as the *life in spirit, our spiritual life form*; and the flesh of man, which is from the Earth, our Mother's side, and what we'll identify as the *life in flesh, our natural life form*. We were created before we were formed, and man's true identity is in the life of his spirit, when he was created; and not of his flesh, when he was formed. The form houses the true identity of man. Man must comprehend that we are spiritual beings first and human beings second.

"So God created man in his own image, the image of God created he him; male and female created he them."(Genesis 1:27)
"And the LORD God formed man of the dust of the ground, and breathed into his nostrils the breath of life; and man became a living soul."(Genesis 2:7)
"Then shall the dust return to the earth as it was: and the spirit shall return unto God who gave it."(Ecclesiastes 12:7)

Once we grasp this concept, we will begin to spiritually align with God and God's Word will align with us. We will begin to know and understand who we are from the very beginning. We were established from the very beginning from the very Word of God.

"In the beginning was the Word, and the Word was with God, and the Word was God."(John 1:1)

Like God, man was from the very beginning. If God is the Word and we are the living truth (***product***) of the Word, then like the Word, we were from the very beginning. Man's comprehension by the sight of his flesh will only limit the capacitation of what he can really see spiritually. In other words, the more man walks by sight and not by faith, he will never truly understand the true identity of himself, nor will he comprehend the truth behind natural occurrences. Faith is having the understanding that your existence is beyond the formed self you see before you. "***Now faith is the substance of things hoped for, the evidence of things not seen.***"**(Hebrews 11:1)** You know that saying, 'you got to have faith'? All this really means is we got to have God, faith in God; because faith is God and God is faith. "***But the fruit of the Spirit is love, joy, peace, longsuffering, gentleness, goodness, faith, meekness, temperance: against such there is no law.***"**(Galatians 5:22-23)** These are qualities of God that can't be undone. God can be no one other than Himself. Mankind having faith is having God within us, it's in our DNA. When the Bible tells us to have faith, the Word is telling us we just simply must have God. In **Numbers 21:8-9**, the story of Moses raising the brass serpent on a pole for an act of faith is no different from Jesus preaching to Nicodemus the Word of faith, which man must believe on Him and that He too must be raised, He says, "***And as Moses lifted up the serpent in the wilderness, even so must the Son of man be lifted up: That whosoever believeth in him should not perish, but have eternal life. For God so loved the world, that he gave his only begotten Son, that whosoever believeth in him should not perish, but have everlasting life. For God*** *sent not his Son into the world to condemn the world; but that the world through him might be saved.*"**(John 3:14-17)** Furthermore, this explains the remnant God is raising in these last days. God is raising radical believers, like myself, to draw all that will believe in Jesus to have faith in God. This is something the Lord shared with me during our time together, 'Moses raised the serpent for the Israelites to believe, Jesus was raised for the Jews to believe, and now the remnant must be raised for the lost, lukewarm Christians and all of mankind to believe.' You see believing is having God in us. When we have God in us, faith is there too, because faith is one of the primary fruits of His Spirit. Faith is the unseen and so is God, that's why the substance of things hoped for (the results), is the evidence (proof) the unseen exists, which is God and what He can provide for you with Him in you. Faith is substance of hope and proof of the invisible. When you accomplish this you are faith, you become faith just as your Father who art in Heaven. If you don't have faith, you don't have God, and it is truly hard to please Him without it.

"*But without faith it is impossible to please him: for that cometh to God must believe that he is, and that he is a rewarder of them that diligently seek him.*"**(Hebrews 11:6)**

Besides love, of all the fruitful qualities of God's Spirit, God's power of faith is what created man and will be the very factor that is needed to sustain man. The evidence of man is the substance of what God hoped for and the proof He exists. We just have to get past our substance of form in order to become completely alive again in the things not seen. We have to be born again of our spiritual selves. Born of the part of our DNA, which connects us back to our Father God in Heaven, submitting to Him the part of ourselves belonging to Mother Earth.

"God's faith is what created us,
and it is man's faith that could destroy us."

"If Abraham were disobedient,
the faith of many nations wouldn't exist."
-Katina Rodgers-

-you are created in His image-

*"And **God said, Let us make man in our image, after our likeness."(Genesis 1:26)** Let's tackle the first part of this statement about image. Image? What image? What does image mean exactly from God's point of view? God's image, of course. I'll be the first to admit it, when I thought of the word image and how man was created in God's image, the first thing that came to my mind was the natural definition of the word image, having shape and form. And so naturally, like any human being, I thought, I looked like God. Especially when growing up, all I saw were different **_idol_** pictures and figures depicting man's image of what they thought Jesus looked like. When we naturally see Jesus in resemblance to mankind, only man's natural thoughts are triggered, and then I beg to ask, whatever happened to activating that spiritual side of us? Growing up I understood my mother's side of my identity, but what ever happened to

our spiritual thinking? What happened to our Father's side? I mean we know He's God, right?

image

You never know how truly smart your younger self was until you begin to reflect on those innocent moments. You know, when I was in my teens I was very careful about certain things I said, along with being careful about certain things I did. I would jokingly say, "I have an image to uphold here," but in all seriousness, I was really serious. Without even thinking or knowing it, maintaining a certain level of standard for us is exactly the man kind of image, God was talking about when He said, "our image". As a teenager, I was on to something true, and I didn't even know it.

I'm being directed here, so I'm going to go here. Earlier I shared my first and only pen pal experience, right? I had no clue what my pen pal looked like, sounded like, or would even be like as a person. All I had to go on was the image she portrayed on paper. I got to learn about the qualities, lifestyle, and character of someone I didn't know. The image my pen pal depicted of herself gave me a pretty good idea of what she was going to be like when I finally met her in person. I'm sure I used my imagination a lot when trying to picture what she looked like. As I'm thinking about it now, while the Holy Spirit is guiding me through this revelation, I didn't need a physical description of her. The physical description or photo of her wouldn't have told me anything about her, it only provided the proof that she existed and the evidence of what she looked like. How else would I have known that was really her anyway? Everything my pen pal wrote on paper was all I needed to know her. With the information I had known, if I were given a day to figure out who my pen pal was in a group of girls, before I physically met her, I could have done it. All I had to do was play with everyone in the group. It didn't matter whether I played with these girls separately, or all at the same time. I just needed to match the description of what I knew about her, when I met her on paper, to what was presented before me in person. Like my pen pal experience, we don't have to see a physical image to know that an image is there. The physical image of a person is just their physical image, it's the essence of that person's presence you'd really want to get to know.

Additionally, the beautiful thing about receiving a revelation from God is, when God reveals, He reveals. God showed me this before, when highlighting the uproar of the whole George Floyd situation…if we didn't have bodies, there would be no discrimination. Light Bulb. **God is Good**!

image of godliness

I think we have enough to go on here to say that we understand when God said, "***Let us make man in our image.***" When God in all His glory and wisdom gives you revelation with the simplest things, who could argue with the results? Now let us make our Heavenly Father really proud and show Him He has created a great work in us. We can and are capable of understanding what He meant about His image. So, what does "***Let us make man in our image***" truly mean? Since we were created in God's image, we must answer this question from that perspective of ourselves, in

God's image. We must answer this question from that perspective of ourselves, in God's image of Godliness. We must answer this question from that perspective of ourselves, in God's image of Spiritual Godliness. Mankind was created in God's image of Spiritual Godliness. Our Father's side of creation, not our Mother's side of formation. And for our sake, I hope we know God is Spirit having no shape or form, for "***No man hath seen God at any time; the only begotten Son, which is in the bosom of the Father, he hath declared him.***"**(John 1:18)** There you have it, scripture tells us only Jesus has seen the Father. I will go into more detail about what Jesus shares with us about our Father later in this series; but for now, we understand we are mini-Me's of God. God created mankind in His image of Godliness for man to commune with Him from Spirit-to-spirit. God-to-god. God to mankind.

The spirit of man is expected to uphold a form of godliness that is in the image of God. Remember when I said, when I was a teenager, I would say, I had an image to uphold. Well, I still do it, but now my life in Christ, my introduction to my You #2, is held to an even higher level of standard, in accordance with the Word, for what I have been chosen to do. I deem it necessary to go here, so I'm going. During my awakening, I have encountered judgment from family, friends and certain people who say they are of Christ, but don't truly know Him to actually say they are of Christ. No worries, I once was a You #1 too, so I truly understand. I only practice righteous judgment and pray! For this reason, we tell our testimonies to help others to awaken and see. Let's put it this way, you wouldn't be reading this book right now had it not been for the introduction to my You #2. Since my awakening, my daily alignment with God and my walk in Christ, I've been living His plans for my promised life. *"**For I know the thoughts that I think toward you, saith the LORD, thoughts of peace, and not of evil, to give you an expected end.**"***(Jeremiah 29:11)**

My awakening was part of God's plan to awaken you, to get you to your promised plan. My development and heightened gift of discernment helped me to filter the You #1's from the You #2's. I found my interaction with people close to me becoming very challenging. We no longer spoke the same language. Almost right away, I noticed my lifestyle change made people ***feel*** uncomfortable, there was this sense of perfectness they felt they must maintain; along with a level of imposed strictness they must abide by, which led them to no longer have the flexibility of ***acting*** the way they were used to. Honestly, I don't feel their pain, but I do understand it, and unfortunately, I have no remorse for it. What I do have remorse for, is worth far more than someone's fleshly feelings. I truly mourn in care of the lost souls and where they will ultimately go if they don't meet their You #2.

your image is equal to your talents
Wow! The Lord is bringing my attention to the scripture about the "Parable of the Talents". **Jesus!** God is not going to give you no more than what you can handle, "***And unto one he gave five talents, to another two, and to another one; to every man according to his several ability.***"**(Matthew 25:15)** I absolutely understand why we are going here.

For you, You #1's who are worried about your current worldly lifestyle, don't worry! God will meet you exactly where you are and help you mature into what He has promised for you. And depending on your talent level (i.e., five, two or one), God will have you walking according to the plans He has purposed for you in no time; and your You #2 will tell you all about it! Once you awaken to understand that there was better for your life all along, you will begin to appreciate the standard to which you were called to walk in. For instance, a pilot or a train operator is held to a higher standard of responsibility for watching the amount of rest they get, and what he or she consumes before operating such transportation. A dog walker, on the other hand, wouldn't have to worry about the level of standard that is required of the pilot or train operator unless they personally chose to. I'm also reminded of this scripture on the subject, ***"But he that knew not, and did commit things worthy of stripes, shall be beaten with few stripes. For unto whomsoever much is given, of him shall be much required; and to whom men have committed much, of him they will ask the more."*(Luke 12:48)** So whether you were ***imprinted*** to be a king, in the U.S. you would be a president; or whether you were born to bathe in the arts, like me, God will meet you. Remember, you are God's creation and your story was written well before you knew about it.

You must know this; God knows what you can handle for what He has promised for you to do. I mean we're talking about God's Promise for your life here, the service description and its functions. The more God knows you can handle, the more He is requiring you to do. Likewise, He's expecting you to refrain from particular habits, as it pertains to sustaining His image for that job description. Look at Samson's promised life, "***For, lo thou shalt conceive, and bear a son; and no razor shall come on his head: for the child shall be a Nazarite unto God from the womb: and he shall begin to deliver Israel out of the hand of the Philistines.***"**(Judges 13:5)** God purposed a promise that was great on Sansom's life for the deliverance of the children of Israel. God had a job that required filling. In **Numbers 6:3,5**, He created a man and needed for him to fulfill the following job description…

MAN NEEDED TO DELIVER ISRAEL

"He shall separate himself from wine and strong drink, and shall drink no vinegar of wine, or vinegar of strong drink, neither shall he drink any liquor of grapes, nor eat moist grapes, or dried" "All the days of the vow of his separation there shall no razor come upon his head: until the days be fulfilled, in the which he separateth himself unto the LORD, he shall be holy, and shall let the locks of the hair of his head grow."

Whether you are helping God to deliver a nation, or your friendly neighborhood, your job description, and standard image requirements will vary from others according to His promised plan for *your* life. You can choose to love Him and walk into the promised plans He has for your life; or you can choose to love the world and continue to walk in the bondages this world afflicts on your life. You can either live to win or you can live to lose. I tell you this, it will be far better to have God help you to walk in His expected image and answer those three questions with you now, than for you to realize from Him later, who you are, where you are from and where you are going for eternity, on that day of judgment.

Sooner or later, mankind must maintain the standard expectation of God's image. *First of all*, this standard was how mankind's expected image of godliness was created to be in the first place, and we should be so honored for Him to think of us this way. *Secondly*, would you want anything less for yourself? And *Third*, we must maintain God's expected standard image ensuring we "**Put on the whole armour of God, that ye may be able to stand against the wiles of the devil.**"**(Ephesians 6:11)** We need this armour to protect ourselves. We must remember anything that's not of God, is the devil; and we don't want to give the devil any rights to our natural or eternal lives. I'm claiming Jesus all day, every day. No matter the level of standard expectation of God's image you are held accountable for by God, you must take a stand, and it must be held for defeating the **_plans_** of the enemy.

God is Holy. God is Sovereign. God is God. God is a Holy, Sovereign, God. If we don't remember anything else, we must remember God's image is Holy, God's image is Sovereign, and God's image is God. When we understand God's image:

we are more likely through the expectation of knowing who He is, to respect who He is; and

we are less likely through the ignorance of assumption to speculate who He is, by the disappointments of who we are;

we are more likely to walk in the understanding of His ways; and

we are less likely to trip in the confusions of our own ways;

we are more likely to walk in the inheritance of holiness, sovereignty, and godliness we were created to love and live in; and

we are less likely to blindside our birthright.

To understand God's image is to know Him. When you are sincerely ready to get to know Him, He'll be the first to reach out to you when He receives the pen pal letter you etched from your heart. From my personal relationship through experience with God, I'd have to say, what I love about His image is His pure essence of being, His authority, boldness, consistency, holiness, godliness, purity, sovereignty, omniscience, power, and truth. It is what He is, what He stands for and He won't fall for anything less; something you will learn and appreciate, after your first heartfelt love letter exchange.

MY TAKEAWAY IN UNDERSTANDING GOD'S IMAGE, IS THAT IT IS ACKNOWLEDGED BEFORE IT IS OVERLOOKED. AS GOD IS HOLY, GOD IS SOVEREIGN AND GOD IS GOD. GOD'S IMAGE IS A HOLY SOVEREIGN GOD.

Everything that we ever need to learn and know about God's Holiness and ourselves, is in the Holy Bible; and so likewise, **I feel it is necessary for us to take a slight detour to learn why the Bible exists. We should know why the Bible was written and what other resources are made available to us from the Word, in order for us to navigate our lives here on Earth.** As a side note, I also feel it is important to mention, just like there is music, there are many reliable God inspired and anointed books, movies, entertainment and retail from other brothers and sisters of truth in the Kingdom of God. God is building His Kingdom on the Earth as it is in Heaven, and so it's time for us to find and support each other. Next, I'm going to expose you to some rude awakening Bible truths.

-your owner's manual-

Basic. Instructions. Before. Leaving. Earth, otherwise known as the Bible. I recently learned this phrase from a Brother in Christ, and I felt the need to share this awesome yet simple way of remembering this truth. The Bible is indeed mankind's owner's manual. The Holy Spirit had to inspire a written manual for mankind, otherwise we'd remain lost. The Holy Bible reveals:

-truths of what God's Spirit is really like when Fathering a fallen mankind;

-an in-depth journal of pen pal letters containing past stories of recounted events and all of the realities mankind needs to know about itself;

-a historical guide of man's triumphs, falls, and patterns of sin cycles;

-tell all information about the future of the Earth and what mankind needs to do to gain their Father's heart; and

-most importantly, the story of a Father's amazing love.

What man fails to realize is that the Bible: i) helps man to stay connected to the part of the DNA we were disconnected from; and ii) supplies disciplinary guidance to that spiritual portion of our DNA that died and fell from God, it is God's parenting handbook for all of mankind. No one is excluded.

Our all-knowing Father provided us with an owner's manual for learning how to partner with Him as we navigate our way through the system of the Earth's world, in hopes that we wouldn't adopt its ways. And since the Earth is the Mother side of our DNA, Adam and Eve's sin has caused her to fall subject to the enemy too. While our Father resides in the third Heaven, a sinful mankind is illegitimately subdued and territorially domiciled on the Earth, and so a handbook was definitely necessary to help us return back home.

A spiritual death occurred when Adam and Eve sinned against God. The sin caused a spiritual malfunction and separation from God. There was no longer a Spirit-to-spirit connection with God. The same way a natural disconnection occurs when a father goes off to war and begins writing letters to his child while he is away. The natural father can communicate anything to his child in those letters. Whether he's expressing his deepest sorrows for missing him or her, or having a way to provide disciplinary instructions. Letters were always a way of communicating in the absence of a natural connection. This is why the Holy Spirit highlighted my pen pal letter experience. The use of letters was the best way to explain God's intentions for inspiring the Holy Bible, since man couldn't naturally see Him. God is not the absent parent here; because God is Spirit, He simply is the invisible parent in this case. And most importantly, it is clear that there was no way for a partially to spiritually dead mankind to know anything about God, their Father, if they continued to operate in the manifested works of their flesh. These manifested works of the flesh are what Paul talks about in **Galatians 5:19-21**, the very works that opposes God just like their father, Satan the devil. "***Ye are of your father the devil, and lusts of your father ye will do. He was a murderer from the beginning, and abode not in the truth, because there is no truth in him. When he speaketh a lie, he speaketh of his own: for he is a liar, and the father of it.***"**(John 8:44)** Jesus was speaking to a group of Jews when He said this. He was simply pointing out their works, the very opposing works that Satan is the father of and what he used to deceive Eve. Mankind was so far from the truth; they couldn't see past the sins of their own flesh. **John 8** speaks true to indicating the times we are in now. Anyone who opposes "***He that is of God heareth God's words: ye therefore hear them not, because ye are not of God,***"**(John 8:47)** is without a doubt a child of this world. When man is naturally more involved in what the world is doing and spiritually less involved in what God is doing, then these very manifestations of their flesh are what will keep man held in the bondage of their sins.

According to our DNA, we were spiritually created in the image and after the likeness of our Father God first, but only naturally formed out of the dust of the Earth second, then logically it should be our primary function to operate under God and not of this world. Unfortunately, Satan's tactical seduction of sin has mankind subdued under his control by a slight malfunction of our spiritual DNA. Jesus said it Himself; Satan was a murderer from the very beginning because when he deceived Eve, he spiritually killed all of us. And the only thing left for Satan to do to have us completely is to kill us naturally before we are born again. Killing off mankind before they're born again is Satan's ultimate goal. The problem for mankind is we are so spiritually blind we can't see it. Earlier when I referenced Jesus' charge to the Jews for their actions, I merely directed your attention to the source of their actions; but this is one of many historical isolated instances where the devil uses man as agents against each other. Sadly, this doesn't even begin to touch the surface of what the devil is capable of and has been getting away with for years. Satan is invisible just like God, and just because he is invisible, it doesn't mean he doesn't exist.

We are truly caught up in a spiritual warfare. There is a real battle going on right now for winning souls between God and Satan the devil. Remember when you go off and do your own works you have to be careful as you are skating on a thin line of good works and worldly works. The worldly works are not of God, but of the devil. You must learn not to partner with the devil on anything, as anything involving the devil can be mistaken as good but is evil; and if God is trying to stop us, we see it as evil when He is really doing us some good.

Earlier in this chapter, we identified you as the reader of this book, and me as the author of this book, right? Suppose you saw several versions of this same book published, which version would you believe is the true version of its original owner? Here you have me the author of this book, then several others who really like the book, but just up and decided they could do a better job of writing it, making it easier to read, easier to understand, and let's say less eye-opening of the truth. Whose book would you believe and whose book would you read? I just described the greatest of the devil's schemes. The devil got slick and inspired other versions of God's Word. Some changes of a few words here and there, some omissions here and additions there and now we have several authors of confusion. For God's Word clearly says, "***For God is not the author of confusion, but of peace, as in all churches of the saints.***"**(1 Corinthians 14:33)** Let's be clear, as long as the King James Version is supporting this book, I'm reciting nothing but the truth.

We need to be reminded that the devil can inspire people too, and if we are not careful to discern our actions, then we are just as easily influenced through his lies, which is exactly how we got here. Having different Bible versions and forms of religion, only allowed us to mistaken good for evil and evil for good. Just because different versions were created for our understanding, it doesn't mean that it is right, it only confirms God's truth about the authors of confusion in **1 Corinthians 14:33**, where it says, "***For God is not the author of confusion, but of peace, as in all churches of the saints.***" Here, God not only points out the difference in the versions, but The King James Version was also written by the man whom God inspired, just like He inspired me to write this book. That Bible is the only version that has an actual name of a living person's name on the book, and he was king, all the rest of the versions were titled according to their authority, which is the author of confusion. Additionally, this scripture points out the peace that will be amongst the churches of the saints who are guided by their obedience to God's voice in accordance with the sound doctrine of the King James Version. Now do you see the difference in good and evil? The devil used us to think we were doing something good when we were in fact creating an evil against ourselves. The devil is seriously trying some soul winning with this one.

When God created us, we were made in His exact image (i.e., authoritative, and wise), after His likeness (i.e., of love, joy, peace, longsuffering, gentleness, goodness, faith, meekness, and temperance) with no flaws. Thus, He didn't make any mistakes. And so, it is evident that before sin, we were once masterminds like our Father, and I believe we still are. I don't think we should have to stoop to undermining our abilities to think. Jesus spoke to us in parables to keep our minds going. If you figure a recording of our history was put in writing, it was because God has given man the ability to naturally see, read, hear, speak, and think, thus, we ought to stop being lazy and start using our God given natural resources, technology and abilities to seek Him. Yes, God gave us a brain to think, because He knew we'd at least have a fighting chance to reach Him through His Word in the King James Version of the Holy Bible.

Okay, besides the fact that we know our Heavenly Father made us to be authoritative and wise like Him, we'll study the fruits of His Spirit in the next section, so that we can really understand what He is like and what it will take for us to walk in our likeness of Him.

-you are created after His likeness-

"***But the fruit of the Spirit is love, joy, peace, longsuffering, gentleness, goodness, faith, meekness, temperance: against such there is no law.***"**(Galatians 5:22-23)**

Alright, so what is God like, what is His likeness? The fruit of God's Spirit is love, joy, peace, longsuffering, gentleness, goodness, faith, meekness, and temperance. Look at all that ***character***! Knowing someone's characteristics is the core of knowing who they are. And so, if I were to ask you, who are you? Start by identifying your core characters, and if you are honest in pinpointing the core characteristics of yourself, you will begin to walk in your truth; and eventually the TRUTH will set you free. Free to walk in your TRUTH with You #2. **Galatians 5:22-23** tells us what our Heavenly Father is like. We now know our Father's likeness, therefore expectations of our likeness should be as our Father's. After learning about God's image, and after His likeness, we should have the complete story in understanding our Father God in His entirety.

I hope you caught on when God said, ***"Let us make man in our image, after our likeness,"*** that God is putting emphasis on making man in His image first, being authoritative and wise; then after His likeness second, being of love, joy, peace, longsuffering, gentleness, goodness, faith, meekness, and temperance. God's image is superior to His likeness of character. It is God's image of being a Holy Sovereign God, which goes hand-in-hand with His likeness, to help us understand His authority. Although, God's likeness is what sets our understanding of knowing who God is and what He is like personally, apart from His image. I got a good one, how many people you know have used this line before? 'I may be a Christian, but I am not a fool?' Plenty of people. And now looking at this from God's perspective, '**I Am meek and loving, but don't let that fool you as to who I AM.**' God's image of commanding authority is superior to His likeness of character in power. Thankfully, even with Himself, God will never allow the powers of His likeable character to ever have control over or supersede the authority of His image; nor will He ever allow the commanding authority of His image to have control over or supersede the powers of His likeness. ***Checks and Balances*** is coming to mind. Remember there will always be a checks and balances system in place to maintain a healthy control of God's image of power and His powers of likeness.

GOD'S IMAGE WILL ALWAYS BE SUPERIOR TO HIS LIKENESS. GOD'S COMMANDING LAWS WERE WRITTEN TO KEEP IN CHECK THE CHARACTERS OF HIS POWERS OF LIKENESS AND IN BALANCE WITH THE AUTHORITY OF HIS IMAGE.

Now, do you want to know what God is like? Meditate on what **Galatians 5:22-23** says to appreciate what Paul wrote, "***But the <u>fruit</u> of the Spirit is love, joy, peace, longsuffering, gentleness, goodness, faith, meekness, temperance: against such there is no law.***" We have to know what Paul is saying here is the truth because, "***All scripture is given by inspiration of God, and is profitable for doctrine, for reproof, for correction, for instruction in righteousness.***"**(2 Timothy 3:16-17)** It is obvious that our Father wanted us to know about Him and what's not of Him; because Paul goes on to tell us what we inherited through sin currently being controlled by our Mother's side of our DNA. "***Now the works of the flesh are <u>manifest</u>, which are these; Adultery, fornication, uncleanness, lasciviousness, idolatry, witchcraft, hatred, variance, emulations, wrath, strife, seditions, heresies, envyings, murders, drunkenness, revellings, and such like: of the which I tell you before, as I have also told you in time past, that they which do such things shall not inherit the kingdom of God.***"**(Galatians 5:19-21)**

the sweet fruits of God's likeness
"But the fruit of the Spirit is love, joy, peace, longsuffering, gentleness, goodness, faith, meekness, temperance: against such there is no law."(Galatians 5:22-23)

What's the first word that comes to mind when you hear the word fruit? Yep, SWEET! Anytime we think of fruit, we think of the mouthwatering taste of its sweet meat, right? When going over in my mind how I was going to word the beginning of this paragraph, I'm reminded of this scripture, *"O taste and see that the Lord is good: blessed is the man that trusteth in him."*(Psalm 34:8) This Psalm of David invites you to come and find out for yourself how good the Lord really is. How sweet really is the fruit of God's Spirit? Well let's find out!

As I said before, God's likeness or in this case, His characters are His powers. There is God's image, which bears the combined power of authority and wisdom; and then we have God's likeness, which are powers of His characters of love, joy, peace, longsuffering, gentleness, goodness, faith, meekness, and temperance. Let me say that again, the fruit of God's Spirit of love, joy, peace, longsuffering, gentleness, goodness, faith, meekness, and temperance are powers of God. God's characters of characteristics are powers. Until revelation, I never really looked at them in that way.

The fruit of the Spirit: love, joy, peace, longsuffering, gentleness, goodness, faith, meekness, and temperance, as defined by Paul, are taken from an online public domain of Webster's Dictionary, 1828 edition.

love

For many years, I honestly took the phrase 'power of love' for granted. In 2020, I watched Ian McCormack's most convincing testimony from the movie "*The Perfect Wave*". At the end of the movie, he describes God's waves of love, and I still didn't get it. I had a sense of what he meant, but I thank God for His divine revelation, because that's when I finally got it. And He simply directed my attention to tel-a-vision superheroes. And oh, now I get it. This is so sad; it goes to show you how brainwashed we are. Especially since I've seen so many "Superman" and "Avenger" movies prior to being born-again. The **_Power_** of Love. The fruit of God's Spirit, His actual characteristics are Powers. HOW COOL IS THAT!

> "***But the fruit of the Spirit is <u>love</u>: against such there is no law.***"

Love: "***To be prompt, free, willing, from leaning, advancing, or drawing forward***. To be ***pleased with***; to ***regard with affection***, on account of some qualities which excite pleasing sensations or desire of gratification. ***To have benevolence of good will for***."

OF ALL OF GOD'S POWERS, LOVE IS THE GREATEST OF THEM ALL. THE ONLY ONE THAT WOULD PROTECT HIS IMAGE OF AUTHORITY. I SEE GOD'S

POWER OF LOVE IN PLACE AS A BALANCING MEANS TO MAINTAIN HIS IMAGE'S ABUSE OF POWER AND AUTHORITY AND AGAINST ANYONE TO CHALLENGE HIS AUTHORITY, ESPECIALLY THOSE WHO FEEL GOD IS AN EVIL, UNJUST, OR UNFAIR GOD. And maybe we have a hard time with God's Authority, because we just don't like authority, "***For the flesh lusteth against the Spirit, and the Spirit against the flesh; and these are contrary the one to the other: so that ye cannot do the things ye would.***" (Galatians 5:17) **THERE YOU HAVE IT; GOD'S POWER OF LOVE IS A MEANS FOR HIS AUTHORITY NOT TO JUST DO THE THINGS IT WOULD. COULD YOU IMAGINE IF GOD's SPIRIT WAS JUST AUTHORITY AND NO LOVE? The answer to this question, humans have been experiencing an imbalance since Adam and Eve sinned. And yet we continue to judge the JUDGE, and continually deny HIS POWER OF LOVE AND HAVE A LACK OF IT THEREOF.**

"***And now abideth faith, hope, charity, these three; but the greatest of these is charity.***"(1 Corinthians 13:13)

When I first read this scripture from the King James Version, I thought, charity, what is charity? I thought the word was love. I looked up charity and there it was, love. Love was within the meaning of God's Word and definition for what He meant. Various authors' meanings for this scripture goes far and wide to show you how easy we've made it for people to have a form of understanding, and yet causing further confusion by changing the true Word of God. I am grateful this happened this way because we get to learn together.

There are revelations after revelations going on right now in real time, as I'm writing this book. I also hope by the time you are reading this book you will receive these revelations too. My prayer is that your eyes are opened to show you the facts. The word 'love', as recorded by other authors of confusion will easily draw man's natural eyes to understanding with their flesh. Look at what I mean from the scriptures listed below. Here's **1 Corinthians 13:13** in the NIV, ESV and NLT, as compared to its original context in the KJV.

"And now these three remain: faith, hope, and love. But the greatest of these is love." NIV

"So now faith, hope, and love abide, these three; but the greatest of these is love." ESV

"Three things will last forever—faith, hope, and love—and the greatest of these is love." NLT

Are you confused? The interpretations are all different. If you read carefully, neither of these scriptures has the same meaning. God showed me the game we played growing up called telephone. The first person would tell the next person the message and by the time it got to the person at the end, the translation was all screwed up. I'd rather take my chances in the King James Version with the benefits of 1. Knowing I'm seeking God through His Word in obedience, because after all it is His Word, and that's all He wants as the author, for us to read His book; and 2. Receiving revelation directly from the author Himself is a bonus.

Showing you the differences in the above scriptures are no different from Satan confusing Eve, then trying the same with Jesus in the wilderness. Sadly today, confusion is playing out according to Satan's plans. These scriptures are not translations, they are interpretations. Automatically when I look at the word 'love', I attach to my feelings of love. When we are looking at the word 'love' in the context of our feelings, immediately we identify with it as something good. Love is a good feeling, right? Love feels good when attached to our feelings. Well, we better get over our feelings, and do it fast! Notice the word feelings. Here's a clue to help with the true translation of this scripture. God is Spirit. When we keep that in the forefront of discerning all scripture, we have a starting point. The core of God's operations is Spirit; and so, the flesh and the feelings thereof are not a consideration of His DNA. We're going to have to get over our feelings; because the word 'love', in this case, is a good word being used as evil in disobedience to God. **HEAR ME. It is the word's misuse that's causing the sin. The works of the flesh are being manipulated, by the word's misuse in sin against God.** *"Woe unto them that call evil good, and good evil; that put darkness for light, and light for darkness; that put bitter for sweet, and sweet for bitter!"*(Isaiah 5:20) Let me tell you right now, fasting is worth the multiple revelations that are **POPPING OFF RIGHT NOW! I DID NOT PLAN THE FLOW OF THIS WRITING, I REPEAT, I DID NOT PLAN THE FLOW OF THIS WRITING. GOD IS GOOD! EARLIER WHEN I ASKED, 'WHEN YOU THINK OF THE WORD FRUIT, WHAT COMES TO MIND', AND THEN TO COME TO THIS SCRIPTURE TO SEE HOW OFTEN WE QUOTE 'GOOD**

FOR EVIL AND EVIL FOR GOOD', BUT NOT CONSIDER THIS PART, 'SWEET FOR BITTER AND BITTER FOR SWEET'. WE'RE TALKING ABOUT GOD'S FRUIT HERE, AND HE IS SWEET! I WANT TO SAY, 'I CAN'T BELIEVE THIS', BUT I CAN'T BECAUSE I CAN BELIVE THIS! **Look how easy sweet becomes bitter when we are confused.** Unknowingly, we will go to great lengths to interpret the Word of God as a bitter taste in our mouths, that we don't realize through our own ignorance of idolatry in these interpretations, we are changing His ways by calling them translations. <u>**This is false!**</u> "*For the flesh lusteth against the Spirit, and the Spirit against the flesh: and these are contrary the one to the other: so that ye cannot do the things that ye would.*"**(Galatians 5:17)**

Now going to the truth, as told in the King James Version by the *real author*, we have the Word 'charity', from the very heart of God's Spirit.

As defined by Webster's Dictionary, 1828 Edition online, Charity **is** love, benevolence, good will; that disposition of heart which inclines men to think favorably of their fellow man, and to do them good. It includes supreme love to God, and universal good will to men.

Notice the word 'Word' is capitalized to show **'charity' is God's Word chosen from His perspective as to what He means regarding love**. He is the author. God's use has a deeper meaning and a broader perspective of relation to one giving of himself in good will to God and all men. The other versions narrow God's perspective to the emotional feelings of the formed man, as opposed to leveling it up to the essence of the man God created. The pure essence of the Holy Spirit's language, led by God's image of authority and wisdom, will never change. When in relationship with God, authority is everything. If He expects it of us, when it comes to His image, then we should expect it of Him, at all times.

With that being said, the Holy Bible, as it was written in the King James Version, defines the truth of God's Word 'charity' in 1 Corinthians 13:13, directing His believers in obedience to the definition of His true **Power of Love**. Anything else is just disobedience, "***Having a form of godliness, but denying the power thereof: from such turn away.***"**(2 Timothy 3:5)**

WOW BIG REVELATION ALERT! I'M SO EXCITED, I HAVE TO YELL IT! YOU ARE NOT GOING TO BELIEVE THIS IS JUST HAPPENING AS I AM TYPING. AS I WAS TYPING *REAL AUTHOR*, AFTER THE KING JAMES VERSION, TO IDENTIFY GOD, THE ONE AND ONLY, TRUE AND LIVING, AUTHOR AND FINISHER, **AND GUESS WHAT, THE WORD AUTHORITY JUST POPPED UP, AS I WAS TYPING THE WORD AUTHOR TO GET THE REVELATION ON THE CONNECTION OF THE TWO WORDS: AUTHOR AND AUTHORITY. AUTHOR IS THE ROOT WORD OF AUTHORITY. GOD'S IMAGE IS DEFINED AS A BEING OF AUTHORITY, AND IN TRUTH, HE IS THE AUTHOR. LET THE AUTHOR TAKE AUTHORITY.** I didn't realize that we were going to go so deep with God's Sweet Fruit of Love, but we did, and I am truly blessed by it. I hope you are blessed by it too!

We're about to learn a lesson in what it means to be deceived for years. **IT'S TIME FOR SOME EXERCISE!**

EXERCISE 3: WE ARE GOING TO PAUSE HERE AND HEAD OVER TO THE WORKBOOK (P.92), TO TEST OUR KNOWLEDGE OF WORD USE.

The affection of love is expected of us in God's Spirit of love, and not the weakness of our flesh. God's Spirit of *Love is a choice, not a feeling*. God's Power of Love is not a feeling. In God's Spirit of love, you don't get to choose to love someone one day, and then feel like hating them the next day. God's Spirit of love is the unconditional choice to love. And if we truly know God in God's Spirit of love, then when we see God's Word of love interchangeably even when used with the Word mercy, we know love. God's Spirit of love is as limitless as He is outside of space and time. God's fruitful Spirit of love signifies a broad spectrum of love above and beyond man's capacity to understand what God's Spirit of love truly is.

When Adam and Eve sinned against God, God in all His Glory and power of love, chose to love beyond the measure of human flesh. God's Spirit of *Love is a choice beyond feeling*. God's Spirit is an expression beyond feelings. **HOLY SPIRIT, HAVE YOUR WAY!** Yeah, that's it! That is the best way to describe God's communicators. Purely intrinsic expression beyond feeling. Every single time, rather than being reactive, God is always very proactive. Scriptures shows us every time. And for this reason, God's charitable contribution of love and compassion toward all of mankind forgives all sins of every kind, shape, and size. All man must do is repent of said sin, and his sin is simply forgotten. We must learn to turn away from said sin and never look back. Oh, now I'm hearing pillar of salt!

"***But God commendeth his love toward us, in that, while we were yet sinners, Christ died for us.***"**(Romans 5:8)**

There is no way for us to truly achieve the true affection of love expected in us on our own. "***For it is God which worketh in you both to will and to do of his good pleasure.***"**(Philippians 2:13)** We are incapable of loving in the Holy Spirit's capacity of love in our own understanding and strength; hence, why we need to comprehend the **<u>sweet</u>** in the fruit of God's Spirit, which is indeed power. Like the scripture says, "***O taste and see that the Lord is good: blessed is the man that trusteth in him.***" We must trust God in order to taste the fruit of His Spirit to acquire its sweetness. God will reward us with His sweetness as He sees growth in us. As we grasp these acquired tastes of understanding, we are to apply these spices to the actions of our own lives. The more we abide in God, the more God abides in us for us to obtain such power. We will see that the Lord is good. We will be blessed when trusting in Him, in His Word, and not the words of others.

The Holy Spirit of God's likeness in Love will always support and prove His image of being a Holy Sovereign God in the total essence of His being a just and righteous God. In short, God's Spirit of Love will always backup God's image of righteous authority. As a final thought, God's image of righteous authority, which is empowered by His sweet likable characteristic of love, will always be proactive and never reactive. Only the flesh is capable of that.

joy

Ok, I'm going to take this as a clue to discuss this in this manner. My spirit is referencing the confusion of joy for happiness. And I see why. Happiness resides on the surface where joy will never be seen. Joy has more of an intrinsic life nestling comfortably on the inside of us. Happiness helps to give joy an expression. Happiness does the work joy otherwise couldn't do from the inside.

> *"But the fruit of the Spirit is <u>joy</u>: against such there is no law."*

Joy: "The passion or emotion ***excited by the acquisition or expectation of good***; that excitement of pleasurable feelings which is caused by success, good fortune, the ***gratification of desire*** or ***some good possessed***, or by a ***rational prospect of possessing*** what we love or desire; ***gladness***; ***exultation***; ***exhilaration of spirits***."

Joy can be expressed more often than we know it, but we will never see it because happiness is allowing for us to see what joy otherwise couldn't. Joy is prompted by the prospect of acquiring something or expecting something good, so whether we have already acquired the 'thing hoped for' or we are expecting it, joy sits from within like a coach making the play calls of our expressions. Joy will make the play call of expression for whatever we are being excited by.

I highlighted some of the play calls in the definition above to give you an idea of what joy looks like from the inside. Think about the times you were excited by something you received or something you expected; had a gratification of desire or a good already obtained; thinking about the possibility of having something; glad; or expressed an exultation or boisterous exhilaration from your spirit. All of these are manifestations of joy. Now when you look at a scripture in the Bible, you will know the appropriate context this word is used in. Let's take a look at a few scriptures:

We'll begin by backing up the joy described in *I Am The 1 Ministries'* mascot scripture **Luke 15:7** with, "***Likewise, I say unto you, there is joy in the presence of the angel of God over one sinner that repenteth.***"**(Luke 15:10)** The angels in heaven are always excited for us, because every day they're either expecting someone to repent or excited because someone already has. The angels are always excited, they are always joyful expressing every play call the COACH expects them to. WE GOT CHEERLEADERS YAL! I mean just think, God already knows, so there's nothing you could do to have God not forgive you for it. The key is to acknowledge it and turn from your ways. And if you haven't done so, signup to take *I Am The 1 Ministries'* **The Color of Grace** exercise to see just how forgiving our Loving Heavenly Father is. The exercise is an inspired exercise, He knows what we need, and He has provided a way for us to come taste and see.

Always have joy in your heart when you are waiting on the Lord or anyone for that matter; have joy in your heart when you are going through a trial; embrace your God given fruit of joy; and have joy in your heart.

Our Heavenly Father goes on further to say, "*I have no greater joy than to hear that my children walk in truth.*"**(3 John 1:4)** I want to bring your attention to the part of the definition where it says, "the *gratification of desire* or *some good possessed*, or by a *rational prospect of possessing* what we love or desire". **HALLELUJAH!** That's an exultation of joy Yal! My heart rejoices in the LORD for desiring us so much! I can almost envision Him now looking down on us or watching however He watches to ensure every assignment is carried out to regain His lost souls.

No confusion there, right? You see how God's scriptures truly come alive when you understand them, God's scriptures speak to you when you activate your power of joy in the Lord. "*For the joy of the Lord is your strength.*" **(Nehemiah 8:10)** God's joy is what is encouraging me, empowering me, giving me the fuel to make it back home. I can honestly say that knowing this 'exhilarates my spirit'. **I'm WANTED!** God wants a wretch like me! His joy brings me joy! When I first learned that I became obsessed, intoxicated in the Spirit of God. And I know if He wants a wretch like me, I know He wants YOU too!

peace

Have you ever literally worried about nothing before? I mean nothing, and I'm not talking about when you were a baby getting waited on hand-and-foot. Well, it wasn't until I met Christ, when I learned the true meaning of PEACE. I mean that true meaning of PEACE. "***And the peace of God, which passeth all understanding, shall keep your heart and minds through Christ Jesus.***"**(Philippians 4:7)** Yeah, that one. That PEACE. Like that newborn baby, not having a care in the world; because all it has to do is open its mouth to communicate to its mother or father for what it wants. That's what I did, when I learned to master the art of having PEACE in my life. By faith, I just opened my mouth, especially since I already possessed the power to have it in the first place; I believe in Him and so I believe I will get what I ask for, and I ask my Father to strengthen me with having PEACE. I know I already have PEACE, but there are some things in life where you'll need an extra dose of God's power for that particular situation. And because I know how it works, I don't let the gas tank ever get too low on having and maintaining my PEACE. The power of PEACE is so well practiced in my life, it drives worried people crazy.

> ***"But the fruit of the Spirit is <u>peace</u>: against such there is no law."***

Peace: "To appease. A state of quiet or tranquility; freedom from disturbance or agitation; applicable to society, to individuals, or to the temper of the mind."

Here's the problem when using the word 'peace' as we operate in it today, it's so overstated, it's underrated. The reason why, we really don't believe in it. We talk-the-talk, but can't even begin to understand what it means to walk-the-walk. Again, we are "*Having a form of godliness, but denying the power thereof: from such turn away.*"**(2 Timothy 3:5)** The only way we are going to activate our inheritance of power is to **stop entrusting in the enemy, and start trusting God FOR A CHANGE**. We must believe in God; we have to believe in the change. I know this may sound cliché, but all we really have to do is just believe.

ONE DAY, I TOLD THE LORD, WE NEED TO BOTTLE THIS UP AND SELL IT! I MEAN, COULD YOU JUST IMAGINE BEING ABLE TO BOTTLE UP PEACE? WE COULD, BECAUSE HE DID, AND GOD ANSEWERS, "I ALREADY HAVE, IT'S INSIDE EACH OF YOU, ALL YOU HAVE TO DO IS JUST BELIEVE."

"Peace I leave with you, my peace I give unto you: not as the world giveth, give I unto you. Let not your heart be troubled, neither let it be afraid."**(John 14:27)** "*For to be carnally minded is death; but to be spiritually minded is life and peace.*"**(Romans 8:6)** "*These things I have spoken unto you, that in me ye might have peace. In the world ye shall have tribulation: but be of good cheer; I have overcome the world.*"**(John 16:33)** "*Therefore being justified by faith, we have peace with God through our Lord Jesus Christ.*"**(Romans 5:1)**

longsuffering

The best way I can naturally describe longsuffering is like having an epidural. When I had an epidural, I knew pain was being inflicted upon me, but I was so numb in the primary areas of childbirth, I didn't feel a thing. And when I say I didn't feel a thing, I'm speaking of the feelings of my enduring flesh. The epidural bought the time of patience for my fleshly response mechanisms of pain to a stable pace of comfort and ease. If you can have a gut punch to your stomach, and you are able to keep your cool without having an epidural or revenge, and still calmly live to talk about it, then congratulations, you have mastered the art of long-suffering.

> ***"But the fruit of the Spirit is <u>longsuffering</u>: against such there is no law."***

Longsuffering: "Bearing injuries or provocation for a long time; patient; not easily provoked."

At best, I'd call longsuffering God's superpower. And lucky for us, it's a good thing too. God is ALL POWERful. If at any time we couldn't bear to see Him, what makes us think, we'd survive His vengeance.

The power most taken for granted is God's longsuffering. Longsuffering is so often misunderstood, because of it, most phrases like this exist:

If God is such a good God, then why does He allow bad things to happen;

You got to stop allowing people to take advantage of you;

Are you just going to let them get away with that;

I don't think _________ is going to happen;

This has been going on for so long;

What denomination are you from;

Thank you for being so patient;

_________ is the true religion;

Things will never change;

I'm reading from the NIV;

Don't stop believing; and

God doesn't exist.

You might be wondering, what do some of these statements have to do with longsuffering. All these statements are very much relevant to longsuffering, especially when they all have to do with God's existence. Longsuffering doesn't mean let's be ignorant to God's existence the same way we can be to Satan's devices. Longsuffering means there is still time for correction. Let's stop Satan's devices by acknowledging God's presence.

"Charity suffereth long, and is kind; charity envieth not; charity vaunteth not itself, is not puffed up, Doth not behave itself unseemly, seeketh not her own, is not

easily provoked, thinketh no evil; rejoiceth not in iniquity, but rejoiceth in the truth; beareth all things, believeth all things, hopeth all things, endureth all things."(1 Corinthians 13:4-8)

gentleness
The first thought that came to mind when looking at the Word gentleness, was seeing a vision of a baby kitten or a parent holding their newborn baby and telling the older brother or sister to be gentle. We apply gentleness when handling something, right? At most, mankind's practice of gentleness stems only from its superficial sensory, when it's really a bit deeper than that. For instance, we are gentle when we find ourselves in the most delicate positions like holding something really fragile, a baby or an egg; but gentleness goes further than the surface, similar to when you issue forgiveness, or even when you help someone with a transgression; as Jesus did in **John chapter 8**, when he assisted the woman who was caught in adultery.

"But the fruit of the Spirit is <u>gentleness</u>: against such there is no law."

Gentleness: "Dignity of birth. Little used. Genteel behavior. Softness of manners; mildness of temper; sweetness of disposition; meekness. Kindness; benevolence. Tenderness; mild treatment."

Man's general use gentleness doesn't have meaning compared to that of God's demonstration of gentleness. When I think of Abba's character of gentleness, I think of

Him applying it to someone's level of brokenness. The same way we would naturally handle a newborn baby, is the same way our Heavenly Father supernaturally handles our brokenness. No matter who they are and what they've done, God's gentleness soothes their heart of brokenness. God's gentleness is consulting all levels of transgressions with the greatest gift of salvation. If you believe in God's gentleness, you are truly free indeed.

The best visual definition of God's gentleness that I can give you is the very last moments of Jesus' life. "***And one of the malefactors which were hanged railed on him, saying, if thou be Christ, save thyself and us. But the other answering rebuked him, saying, dost not thou fear God, seeing thou art in the same condemnation: And we indeed justly; for we receive the due reward of our deeds: but this man hath done nothing amiss. And he said unto Jesus, Lord, remember me when thou comest into thy kingdom. And Jesus said unto him, verily I say unto thee, today shalt thou be with me in paradise.***"**(Luke 23:39-43)** These iconic moments are exemplary of God's gentleness because even up until the point of death for both Jesus and the sinner, God is still merciful in forgiveness of sins. And like His Father, Jesus was still working, ministering to a sinner until death.

"I can of mine own self do nothing: as I hear, I judge: and my judgement is just; because I seek not mine own will, but the will of the Father which hath sent me."
(John 5:30)

Mankind's attempt at gentleness needs serious improvement. As fleshly beings, naturally we gravitate more toward living in gentleness from our Mother's perspective, and not from the spiritual perspective of our Heavenly Father. After grasping the Spirit's true fruit of gentleness, we need to do an evaluation of what it will take to begin making a 180 degree turn toward a genuine walk in that direction. Simply put, having a lifestyle of gentleness is daily living in subtle applications of charity.

goodness
"And God saw every thing that he had made, and, behold, it was very good. And the evening and the morning were the sixth day."(Genesis 1:31)

> "If God saw that every thing He made was very good,
> then who are we to complain?"
> -Katina Rodgers-

We have done a great job of allowing our pride to undermine our character of goodness. I mean, we are never sincerely happy with just good, because good is never good enough. For instance, let's take the scripture **Genesis 1:31**, where God saw every thing that he made and said it was very good. And if God saw that every thing He made was very good, then who are we to complain? I mean really, men are some of the most complaining, never satisfied people. You name it, it's never good enough. How unfortunate, that in **Genesis 1:3**, the light of mankind, the very essence God created to help save the world in these last days; God said *"it was good"*, and every thing including the very thing, the formation of man's body, God says *"it was very good"*. Not just good, but very good. And for some crazy reason, we're not satisfied with the actual looks and features He has given us. Demoralizing the creation of the Creator is a slap in the face to say the least. Mankind is at the top of the invention chain of existence, and the only ones not satisfied with the Creator's creation. For something that couldn't even exist without the Creator, mankind has immediately become an expert of knowing the quality of good; and we've quickly become a poor example of being good. Unfortunately, we acquired this sin from its father, Satan the devil. Here we are telling the Creator, He could have done better. Not good, not very good, but better.

> **"But the fruit of the Spirit is <u>goodness</u>: against such there is no law.**"(Galatians 5:22-23)

Goodness: "The state of being good; the physical qualities which constitute value, excellence or perfection; as the goodness of timber; the goodness of soil."

Another tactic of the devil's devices when operating in goodness, is having man use good to their advantage, while taking advantage of good. This right here is an easy sinner. For example, the good man often engages in warrants some form of reward. The seed originally placed in man's heart wasn't necessarily for someone else, it was always for himself. The charity disguised as love was never really there in the first place. When man goes to the length of claiming to sew a deed into someone else that is ultimately for himself, he most certainly does not love his neighbor and neither does he love himself. In fact, he is loving his neighbor as he loves himself, as a liar. The type of love comprehended here is lying to himself and others. Man would have to do good and walk away from it in order for it to be considered a charity. If the intent is to get a reward, then goodness is no longer good.

For goodness' sake, mankind's state of being must come into agreement with goodness for either of them to truly exist.

"*Let love be without dissimulation. Abhor that which is evil; cleave to that which is good.*"(Romans 12:9)

"The response to a man's goodness exposes the truth in his heart." -Katina Rodgers-

faith
Of all of the fruits of the Spirit, faith is a big one. Faith is the key ingredient to connecting mankind back to its original heritage of its Father's side of the family. Faith has repeatedly proven throughout history, man's failure to believe. And fortunately, God's requirement of faith is all we need. Faith is believing, and believing is faith. In a nutshell, we just have to believe. When we believe in God, we magnify all He is, all He does and all we are in Him by our faith in Him, to provide what we hope for, which is the very proof of His existence, the unseen. **Hebrews 11:1**

"Our hope is the life support to our faith; and our faith is the glorification to our supporter."
-Katina Rodgers-

*"**But the fruit of the Spirit is <u>faith</u>: against such there is no law.**"*

Faith: "To trust; to persuade, to draw towards any thing, to conciliate; to believe, to obey."

*"**For we walk by faith, not by sight.**"***(2 Corinthians 5:7)** This scripture has become such a cliché. It is the very Word of God that loses its power over time; especially, in the hearts of those who don't believe or just don't believe in the scripture. I think people just like to say it...they like the way it sounds as it rolls off their tongues. After all, it is a scripture that makes one appear to be wise and have it all together. In actuality, this scripture possesses the power of faith, if one would only believe in it. This scripture is the 'exit' sign of all doorways. Like all doorway 'exit' signs, they are clear, concise and leads directly to the point. For, if we walk by faith, and not by sight, we too, will have to trust that God's Word will not return to Him void.

*"**He only is my rock and my salvation: he is my defence; I shall not be moved,**"***(Psalm 62:6)**

On October 25, 2021, I released an announcement for *I Am The 1 Ministries'*, The Color of Grace exercise. Prior to the announcement, I had been building up the advertisement, putting on the final touches and boasting about God's goodness on this wonderful exercise; but to no avail, not too many people have a care for seeing what God is doing for them. Fear is ramped-up on high demand in the people of this world. And naturally, because of it, I have some thoughts of discouragement come through for their lack of interest. I'm trying really hard to understand why my working so hard to help save other people's lives isn't the same for them to save their own. Like many of my brothers and sisters of Light, we fight, we tirelessly fight, and try to understand the inability for people to wake up to what's going on around us all. The thought that was going on in my head, as one of the remnant being raised to be a servant of the Lord; why wasn't anyone listening, no one is interested, and the conditions, the hold, the strongholds, the brainwashing, the bondage, the oppressive ways of this world really has the people deceived to think that this world is indeed their savior.

Then the Lord brings this to my attention, He compares the general fear of COVID to the Israelites fear of the fiery serpents in **Numbers 21:4-9**. "*And they journeyed from mount Hor by the way of the Red sea, to compass the land of Edom: and the soul of the people was much discouraged because of the way. And the people spake against God, and against Moses, wherefore have ye brought us up out of Egypt to die in the wilderness? for there is no bread, neither is there any water; and our soul loatheth this light bread. And the Lord sent fiery serpents among the people, and they bit the people; and much people of Israel died. Therefore the people came to Moses, and said, We have sinned, for we have spoken against the Lord, and against thee; pray unto* *the Lord, that he take away the serpents from us. And Moses prayed for the people. And the Lord said unto Moses, make thee a fiery serpent, and set it upon a pole: and it shall come to pass, that every one that is bitten, when he looketh upon it, shall live. And Moses made a serpent of brass, and put it upon a pole, and it came to pass, that if a serpent had bitten any man, when he beheld the serpent of brass, he lived.*" The understanding that was downloaded in my spirit was that whosoever believes will take part in The Color of Grace exercise by faith will be saved. Whoever He sends out, what I mean is, who God has called to be a servant of the Lord in this hour, to reach people who are engaged by faith, the remnant He has raised like Moses raised the serpent and whoever believes by faith upon what God is doing through them will be saved. It's that simple. The discouragement that I have comes from my concern for the people I'm speaking to, family, relatives near and far, people who are supposedly Christians or at least believe in God, close friends and neighbors. There is no interest at all in what I'm saying or doing. I could yell my brains out and it would make no difference to them. I'm concerned about the unforeseen outcome. My experience through the Lord's calling on my life and His Word from the Bible are the only reliable sources to believe as grounds for what I believe in, but not everybody believes. For all these years, I'm not sure why so-called believers shoved the Bible in everybody else's faces, but in these last couple of years, all of a sudden, the Word just doesn't apply to them for some reason. WELL, I'LL BE.

After much pondering over this thought **Romans 9** comes upon my spirit. This chapter is ironically depicting Israel's Rejection of Christ. I can't make this stuff up. I honestly don't know the Bible like many people who has studied for years, but by relationship and revelation, you will learn by supernatural speed.

As usual, I read the entire chapter. In reading the beginning, **verses 1-5**, I feel as if Paul's words were that of my own. You know that with and in your heart of hearts you are functioning under the operation of the true and living God. I mean the God lives, Jesus speaks, and the Holy Spirit moves, God. Yeah, that One! And no one believes you. No one believes in the true and living God, but they do believe in a god. I don't think they know which one though. Paul wishes he was accursed as the people were. I guess he says, hey, if you can't beat them, then you might as well join them. I don't have the same wishes, but sometimes I do wonder what is it that people see on the other side. With the understanding of Satan's authority over this worldly system, I don't need to be there, I understand it enough not to want to be there.

And when I continue reading on into **verses 6-13**, acquiring some further understanding from *bibleref.com*, these verses reads that God's Word is God's Word. Even though God's Word is what it is, not all of Israel, His chosen people by conception or the faith, will choose God. That is it! Period. We have to understand that not all people are going to choose God. God knows this, but people like Paul and myself can't seem to understand and grasp this concept. We just want to save everybody. Now, it's in **verses 11-13** that really has my attention, because I was there before. I believe due to my continual dwelling upon this misunderstanding, my Heavenly Father has me here again, this time for my need to thoroughly understand it, so that I can move on.

This is crazy, because I understood this before, but the first time this manna went right over my fleshly head and didn't seep into my spirit as it should have. This time around, we are going to make it stick. **Verses 11-13** goes like this, "***(For the children not yet being born, neither having done any good or evil, that the purpose of God according to election might stand, <u>not of works</u>, but of <u>him that calleth;)</u>*** it was said to her, The elder shall serve the younger. <u>As it is written, Jacob I have loved, but Esau I have hated</u>.**"

In these verses Paul speaks about when God made a decision between the two of Rebecca's sons as to whom would be a people of 'Him who calls'. It wasn't about right or wrong, good or evil, but simply about God making a choice as He wills. The decision foretells who God loves more by their faith and because of their faith who He still loves more, even today. We are all loved, but for those who walk and live by faith are loved all the more and are highly favored.

Not of works, the Esau's, the church, the sight walkers, the touchables, do'ers and seekers of the law and of this world according to what they see and do in the world by leaning on their own understanding.

Him who calls, the Jacob's, the remnant, the faith walkers, the untouchables, the workers and see'ers of the Kingdom in the spirit according to what they spiritually sense from the Kingdom about this world; justified by obedience of their works through trust in God with all their heart, acknowledging God in all their ways by allowing Him to direct their paths in all their ways.

Like Abraham, our father of faith, our works are determined accordingly, by the obedience of our faith. Our works are performed in accordance with our call to obedience, trust and faith in God. IN SUMMARY, OUR WORKS ARE THE PRODUCTS OF ACTING IN THE OBEDIENCE, WHICH IS LED BY FAITH AND FOLLOWED BY OUR TRUST IN 'HIM WHO CALLS' US.

EXAMPLE: WHEN 'HIM WHO CALLS', CALLS YOU, AND YOU ARE LIKE, DO I TRUST YOU? AND THEN YOU SAY, ALL RIGHT, I'M GOING TO DO THIS, I'M GOING TO STEP OUT ON FAITH ON THIS ONE, AND DO EXACTLY EVERYTHING YOU TELL ME TO DO, NO MATTER WHAT THE COST, I'M GONNA TAKE YOUR WORD FOR YOUR BOND ON THIS ONE, AND WE GONNA SEE WHAT HAPPENS.

FAITH WITHOUT WORKS IS DEAD. FAITH WITHOUT BEING OBEDIENT TO THE VOICE INSTRUCTING YOU TO GET THE WORKS DONE, IS DEAD. DISOBEDIENCE IS DIVINATION, AND DIVINATION IS NOT GOD. WITH THE RESPONSIBILITY OF FAITH MUST COME THE WORKS IN OBEDIENCE TO GOD. THESE WORKS ARE NOT OUR OWN. AND AS SUPERNATURALLY AS THEY ARE, THEY COULD NEVER BE DONE ON OUR OWN, IN THE NATURAL.

WE HAVE TO UNDERSTAND THAT IT IS BY OUR CHOICES, WHICH DECIDES WHETHER WE ARE A PART OF GOD'S CHOSEN OR NOT. WE DECIDE, GOD JUST MADE THE DECISION TO SET THE STANDARDS. THERE ARE TWO CATEGORIES WHICH DISTINGUISHES THE STANDARDS UNDER WHICH AN INDIVIDUAL FALLS. THE STANDARDS OF THESE CATEGORIES ARE DEFINED BY BIBLICAL PRINCIPLES. YEP, THE MANUFACTURER'S SET OF INSTRUCTIONS ON HOW TO OPERATE IN THE SYSTEM OF THIS WORLD. THE VERY OWNER'S MANUAL WE ARE TO DEFER TO, TO HELP US GUIDE OUR LIVES. THE VERY WORD THAT WAS FROM THE BEGINNING.

GOD MADE THE CHOICE FOR YOU TO DECIDE YOUR SIDE. HE'LL STILL LOVE YOU NO MATTER WHAT SIDE YOU ARE ON, BUT HIS LOVE IS MORE FAVORED TO THOSE WHO CHOOSE HIM BY FAITH.

"WORKS IS AN ACT OF CHARITY, SOLELY GUIDED BY THE OBEDIENCE OF ONE'S FAITH. ANYTHING ELSE IS FAIR GAIN."
-Katina Rodgers-

meekness
WHO DOES GOD CHOOSE? THE BIBLE SAYS, *"Blessed are the meek: for they shall inherit the earth."***(Matthew 5:5)** Through the Spirit of Faith, God made man and by that same Spirit of Faith, God chose His people. Now, if we have learned anything from this example, we should understand how God expects for us to make the same decision when it comes to choice, and what we should choose. The choice we must make concerning living life here on Earth ultimately leading to our eternal lives in Heaven. The choice is ours to choose love, and to choose love is to choose Him.

And so now, through the Spirit of meekness, we learn the identity of who God chooses. The choice of God's chosen people is based on an inherited character of their DNA. Of the 9 fruits of God's Holy Spirit, meekness is not only a power of God, but unbeknownst to mankind, meekness is a true natural quality imbedded in the spiritual DNA of the chosen children of God. Who knew meekness would be man's superpower. I don't know if I'll be the first to call being mild temper and not often speaking up as a superpower; but God chose who would naturally carry His DNA trait of meekness for a reason, and I'm sure glad I'm one of them.

"But the fruit of the Spirit is <u>meekness</u>: against such there is no law."

WHAT IS MEEK?

NOAH WEBSTER'S ONLINE 1828 DICTIONARY DEFINES MEEK AND MEEKNESS AS THIS:

Meek, **1.** Mild of temper; soft; gentle; not easily provoked or irritated; yielding; given to forbearance under injuries. **2.** Appropriately, humble, in an evangelical sense; submissive to the divine will; not proud, self-sufficient or refractory; not peevish and apt to complain of divine dispensations.

"Now the man Moses was very meek, above all the men which were upon the face of the earth."(Numbers 12:3)

"Take my yoke upon you, and learn of me; for I am meek and lowly in heart: and ye shall find rest unto your souls."(Matthew 11:29)

Meekness, Softness of temper; mildness; gentleness; forbearance under injuries and provocations. 1. In an evangelical sense, humility; resignation; submission to the divine will, without murmuring or peevishness; opposed to pride, arrogance and refractories.

"Meekness, temperance: against such there is no law."(Galatians 5:23)

"Moreover, brethren, I would not that ye should be ignorant, how that all our fathers were under the cloud, and all passed through the sea."
(1 Corinthians 10:1)

"Meekness is a grace which Jesus alone inculcated, and which no ancient philosopher seems to have understood or recommended."
webstersdictionary1828.com

WHO ARE THE MEEK?

TO LIST A FEW OF THEIR QUALITIES, THE MEEK ARE LOWLY, A LOW TEMPERED PEOPLE WHO TEND TO STAY TO THEMSELVES; AT TIMES THEY CAN BE SHY; QUIET; NORMALLY NOT LIKELY TO MAKE THE FIRST MOVE TO TALK TO SOMEONE ELSE UNLESS THEY KNOW THEM OR DEPENDING ON THE SITUATION; AND THEY ESPECIALLY ENJOY STAYING IN THE BACKGROUND. THE MEEK DON'T TEND TO SPEAK UP IN SURROUNDING SITUATIONS OR FOR THEMSELVES AS OFTEN AS THEY SHOULD, WHEN THEY SHOULD. THE MEEK SEEM WEAK AND EASY TO PUSH OVER. THEY DON'T TEND TO COMPLAIN AND WILL ALLOW THEMSELVES TO GET HURT BEFORE THEY WILL ALLOW FOR SOMEONE ELSE TO GET HURT. THE MEEK ARE HELPFUL TO OTHERS. THEY ARE SUBMISSIVE TO AUTHORITY AND ARE OPPOSED TO PROUD AND VAIN LIVING.

WHO ARE YOU? Do you have the character trait of meekness? Are light bulbs flashing off and on right now. Is any of this starting to make sense from a spiritual perspective? Having an understanding of this information most certainly doesn't mean anyone has to have a degree in rocket science to figure out this goes further than "*23 And Me*". God has made a way through the terms I coin, the "Trinity And Me" or the "Trinity In Me", for you to discover whether you have your Heavenly Father's character or not.

IT'S TIME FOR SOME EXERCISE!

EXERCISE 4: WE ARE GOING TO PAUSE HERE AND HEAD OVER TO THE WORKBOOK (P.110) TO LOOK AT EACH DEFINITION AGAIN. DO YOU CONSIDER YOURSELF TO HAVE THIS QUALITY OF MEEKNESS? IF SO, LIST 3 TRAITS THAT YOU HAVE BY DEFINITION OF THIS CHARACTER AND GIVE YOUR TESTIMONY FOR EACH TRAIT IN ACTION.

AND WHY WILL THE MEEK INHERIT THE EARTH?

THE MEEK WILL INHERIT THE EARTH, BECAUSE IN GOD'S EYES THE MEEK ARE MORE LIKELY TO SAVE THE LOST SOULS OF THE EARTH. THE MEEK ARE THE ONES WHO POSSESS THE EXACT PURE TRAIT OF GOD'S DEFINING CHARACTER. MEEK IS WHO HE IS. HENCE, THE MEEK'S TEMPERMENT AND UNDERSTANDING OF LIFE WILL SAVE A LOST SOUL, BECAUSE THEIRS ARE ALREADY SAVED. THE MEEK PERSON WILL SAVE ITSELF AND THEIR ENEMY.

THE ASSIGNMENT OF THE MEEK IS TO SAVE THE LOST SOULS BEFORE MAKING THEIR WAY BACK HOME. THE LOST SOUL AWAKENS TO COMPREHEND WHAT HAS HAPPENED, WHICH CAUSES THEM TO ADOPT THE SAME CHAIN REACTION OF GRATITUDE. HAVING A SPIRIT OF MEEKNESS IS AN ABSOLUTE NECESSARY PERSONALITY TO ACQUIRE THE SOULS GOD DESIRES FOR HIS KINGDOM.

THINK ABOUT IT, A LOOSE CANON WILL TAKE OUT ANY AND EVERY BODY IT CAN AND WILL, INCLUDING THEMSELF. WHILE ON THE OTHER HAND, YOU HAVE SOMEONE WHO IS MILD MANNERED TO HAVE THE NECESSARY PATIENCE AND SUPERPOWER TO DIFUSE THE SITUATION. THUS, SAVING MORE LIVES AND STOMPING THE DEVIL IN HIS TRACKS. WHEN SOMEONE POSSESSES THE HOLY SPIRIT'S SUPERPOWER OF MEEKNESS, THEY MAKE THEIR TERRITORIES A THREAT TO THE DEVIL, WHICH BECOME A NO SOULS FOR SATAN SAFETY ZONE.

"But God hath chosen the foolish things of the world to confound the wise; and God hath chosen the weak things of the world to confound the things which are mighty."(1 Corinthians 1:27)

"But the fruit of the Spirit is love, joy, peace, longsuffering, gentleness, goodness, faith, meekness, temperance: against such there is no law."(Galatians 5:22-23)

"But the meek shall inherit the earth; and shall delight themselves in the abundance of peace." (Psalm 37:11)

"But let it be the hidden man of the heart, in that which is not corruptible, even the ornament of a meek and quiet spirit, which is in the sight of God of great price." (1 Peter 3:4)

"Put on therefore, as the elect of God, holy and beloved, bowels of mercies, kindness, humbleness of mind, meekness, longsuffering."(Colossians 3:12)

"To speak evil of no man, to be no brawlers, but gentle, shewing all meekness unto all men."(Titus 3:2)

"The meek also shall increase their joy in the Lord, and the poor among men shall rejoice in the Holy One of Israel."(Isaiah 29:19)

"That ye may be blameless and harmless, the sons of God, without rebuke, in the midst of a crooked and perverse nation, among whom ye shine as <u>lights</u> in the world."(Philippians 2:15)

> "The meek will carry the light.
> The meek will carry the load."
> -Katina Rodgers-

temperance
I was stuck on how to approach this subject matter until my husband came home from work to see that, in addition to me working on this book, I washed the bedding. My

husband's whole demeanor changed from honey I'm home to what happened to the bed. And to think I was stuck writing on the subject of patience. Now that I'm thinking about it, it's funny. I was inquiring of the Holy Spirit about His Spirit of temperance; and thinking about it even more, I realized I got impatient myself. The Lord waited as the plot thickened. And since I didn't even wait to hear anything, I figured I'd just go around the subject and come back to it a little later. Little did I know that both mine and my husband's impatience, during this day of writing about patience was the exact example I needed to write about patience. **"Ye stiffnecked and uncircumcised in heart and ears, ye do always resist the Holy Ghost: as your fathers did, so do ye."(Acts 7:51)** This is such a shame, I truly need to learn from this. I repent!

You would have thought someone stole the bed to keep him from getting into it, because that's exactly what happened. After dinner and a shower, the best part happened to be the worst part. All it took was for us to start making the bed. No justice, no peace. He complained every step of the way. He didn't want to put the pillowcases on. In fact, he said "I don't even know why you bought pillows, I don't need pillows." THE DEVIL IS A LIAR, because he would be the first one on my side of the bed sleeping on my pillows. He grunted and groaned the whole way making up that bed. No patience whatsoever. And the Lord shows me how much we lack temperance, take His patience for granted, and each other's, for that matter. And this is what I wound up telling my husband while making up the bed. 'Any other time you would have no idea when I have laundered and remade the bed. I don't complain while making it, I take my time getting the bed done. You on the other hand are able to come home, shower, have dinner and head off to la-la-land, with no thanks given.' As I was speaking this to my husband, I saw it from God's perspective on how we take God for granted in our impatience. First-off, our ignorance and lack of understanding as to what it takes behind the scenes and second, there is never a genuine thank you for it being done. **JESUS, JESUS, JESUS, GOD PLEASE FORGIVE ME.**

When we stand before the judgment seat of God, our lives are used to testify against us. Seeds of unforgiveness will be the first accusation against us and our lack of patience will be right behind it. What can I say, it is truly unfortunate how we lack patience. And there are those moments we all have in our lives of testing God's patience with us, which is why I believe the fruit of temperance bears witness to God's Spirit of meekness, proving the loving and merciful God He is. By far these two fruits are true compliments of each other, they must work together, absolutely hand-in-hand.

Without a doubt, I know I have the qualities of meekness, but my patience slightly begs to differ. I owe my lack of making the best choices when interacting with the elements of this world to my default of impatience. Although, I'm truly blessed to testify, "***But now, O Lord, thou art our father; we are the clay, and thou our potter; and we all are the work of thy hand.***"***(Isaiah 64:8)*** Who alone but God is more qualified to assist us in bettering ourselves with keeping calm, having more patience, and slowing down.

We could learn a lot about temperance if we just whole heartedly study the Word. There is such great history in the Bible and much to learn from our ancestors' lack of temperance and our Heavenly Father's power of it thereof. Having the blessings of this quality is much more than an advantage for ourselves, but a great benefit for others.

> **"But the fruit of the Spirit is <u>temperance</u>:
> against such there is no law."**

Temperance: "Patience; calmness; sedateness; moderation of passion."

> "Patience is like a flower
> waiting for the sun to go down."
> -Katina Rodgers-

your power of likeness infiltrated
"But the fruit of the Spirit is love, joy, peace, longsuffering, gentleness, goodness, faith, meekness, temperance: against such there is no law."(Galatians 5:22-23)

We all grew up watching the world's infamous superheroes with all their fictitious superpowers, then at some point or another wishing we had them ourselves, because that's how believable they were to us. Even the possibilities of being an invisible man infiltrated our minds at some point. Welp, back in Adam and Eve's day, Satan used a serpent as a voice box, when he presented Eve with the idea that she didn't have something she already had. Fast forward to where we are now, Satan has done it again and has been doing it for years with the tel-a-vision. The Bible forewarns us about the prince of the airways in **Ephesians 2:2** saying, "***Wherein in time past ye walked according to the course of this world, according to the prince of the power of the air, the spirit that now worketh in the children of disobedience.***" Years and years of indoctrination infiltrated in the minds of mankind, and we're still allowing the devil to get away with it all. The prince of the power of the airways will stop at nothing to deceive us. Satan and all of his demons are using their powers and everything within the powers of the airways at their disposal to continue to destroy us. And so, the question is, how has it come to the point that we've allowed the invisible wonders of our Creator and His power to slip through our minds, to believe what isn't, over what actually is? Unfortunately, mankind's crazy beliefs surrounding God's existence, not only denies His power, but it leaves us exactly where we are today, powerless.

"***Having a form of godliness, but denying the power thereof: from such turn away.***"(2 Timothy 3:5)

In the long, but short of it, when we allow an infiltration of our minds, we covet to an agreement with the enemy. As soon as we allow him to have us believing in something that he authored, then we are now followers and believers of him and not of God. WE UNKNOWINGLY UNFRIENDED GOD. This is a good example of what I believe Brother Whitfield Harrington calls the bait and switch. In other words, as soon as we agree to something that doesn't align with the Word of God or doesn't align with who God is, then not by default, but by choice, we choose to be fathered by the god of this world as opposed to being Fathered by our True and living God in Heaven. According to the laws of Heaven, anything that we allow to enter into our eye-gates, ear-gates, mouth-gates, and even the gates of our homes, that is not of God, we have just given the enemy legal rights to our lives and the lives of our family. Therefore, we become the ownership of the devil, we become a slave to these sins, thus now bearing all the consequences of these sins. We are so asphyxiated on our earthly rights, that we don't even know our Heavenly rights. It's the rights we have in Heaven that have seniority over the rights we have here on Earth. In fact, how we live here on Earth determines how Heaven rules in our favor. The problem with that is, since we don't know these Heavenly rights, we make the assumption that we can have a covenant with the devil and still claim to be a child of God. IT DOESN'T WORK THAT WAY! IT NEVER HAS, AND IT NEVER WILL! We have to make a choice, it's either one or the other. For "*No man can serve two masters: for either he will hate the one, and love the other; or else he will hold to the one, and despise the other. Ye cannot serve God and mammon.*"(Matthew 6:24)

"THE EARTH IS THE LORD'S, AND THE FULLNESS THEREOF; THE WORLD, AND THEY THAT DWELL THEREIN. FOR HE HATH FOUNDED IT UPON THE SEAS, AND ESTABLISHED IT UPON THE FLOODS. WHO SHALL ASCEND INTO THE HILL OF THE LORD? OR WHO SHALL STAND IN HIS HOLY PLACE? HE THAT HATH CLEAN HANDS, AND A PURE HEART; WHO HATH NOT LIFTED UP HIS SOUL UNTO VANITY, NOR

SWORN DECEITFULLY. HE SHALL RECEIVE THE BLESSING FROM THE LORD, AND RIGHTEOUSNESS FROM THE GOD OF HIS SALVATION. THIS IS THE GENERATION OF THEM THAT SEEK HIM, THAT SEEK THY FACE, O JACOB."(Psalm 24:1-6)

WE MUST REMEMBER that the earth is the Lord's, the fullness and those that dwell therein. The earth, the fullness and those that dwell therein were created by God's will; and you best believe that by God's will, He will have His way.

"And he said to them all, if any man will come after me, let him deny himself, and take up his cross daily, and follow me."(Luke 9:23)

FOR YEARS, THE ENEMY HAS BEEN DECEIVING US INTO AGREEING TO THINGS THAT ARE NOT OURS, AND AGREEING TO WANTING THINGS WE ALREADY HAVE. GOD, OUR CREATOR, DELIGHTS IN US AND RIGHTFULLY SO, HE HAS GIVEN TO US ALL THINGS WE COULD EVER THINK OR ASK. WE ALREADY HAVE POWER. WE JUST HAVE TO WAKE UP AND TAKE IT! **PLEASE WAKE UP!**

"BUT MY GOD SHALL SUPPLY ALL YOUR NEED ACCORDING TO HIS RICHES IN GLORY BY CHRIST JESUS."(Philippians 4:19)

your works identifies your likeness
We must understand that in all of God's Spirit of invisibility, so are His powers, the very fruit of His Spirit in love, joy,

peace, longsuffering, gentleness, goodness, faith, meekness, and temperance. And so, if His powers are invisible when He is using them, then don't you think they'd be invisible when we are using them too? "*For we walk by faith, not by sight.*"(**2 Corinthians 5:7**) We shouldn't be looking for the power of these spiritual fruits to be seen. Unfortunately for mankind, we do a poor job of this. Always wanting something we've done to be noticed. "*Shall not God search this out? For he knoweth the secrets of the heart.*"(**Psalm 44:21**) Each of these powerful fruits are invisible and never will be seen. It is the works accomplished through them which give these fruits of power their visibility; and depending on the intent in which these works are performed, so by these works we will be judged. Therefore, make no mistake of God's meaning for works, specifically when it comes to the intentions of your heart for doing them. The beauty of walking in faith with these spiritual fruits allows for them to work with you from the inside out. Remember, the characteristics of these fruitful powers are an expression of in-depth meaning that is most certainly not superficial. So, when expressing love, it doesn't necessarily mean there is a need to create a scene for it to be seen, acting on the choice we made to do so is all that matters.

IT'S TIME FOR SOME EXERCISE!

EXERCISE 5: WE ARE GOING TO PAUSE HERE AND HEAD OVER TO THE WORKBOOK (P.116) TO LOOK AT 3 SPECIFIC MEANINGS WE HAVE FOR WORKS, TO ENSURE WE HAVE THE PROPER UNDERSTANDING IN

DIFFERENTIATING THE WORKS OF MAN VS THE WORKS OF GOD.

Now, I hope that we have the understanding needed to identify works as it is seen in the eyes of God. For our works are vital to identifying who we are, as they are made known by the fruit they come from. That's why I felt the need to touch on the sweet fruits of God's likeness in this section, additionally, it was an essential introduction to the next chapter. Please note that touching on these fruits was only an introduction and doesn't even begin to skim the surface of who God is; although, it was very necessary to identify the fruit of God's Spirit as they are the actual blueprint of our spiritual souls. And for this reason, it is important to understand that the fruits of our character are invisible, and yet they are exactly the powerful actions of who we are; and depending on how they are used, they can either be intentionally seen or humbly noticed.

REMEMBER TO BE MINDFUL OF THE POWER OF YOUR CHARACTER. YOUR CHARACTER HAS POWER. YOUR CHARACTER IS POWER. THE USE OF YOUR CHARACTER'S POWER WILL BE JUDGED ACCORDING TO THEIR WORKS. THERE ARE HEAVENLY LAWS IN PLACE TO MAINTAIN THE CONTROL OVER THE LIKENESS OF OUR CHARACTER, SO THAT THE LIKENESS OF OUR CHARACTER WILL BE IN SUBMISSION TO OUR IMAGE. AND IF AT ANY TIME, OUR CHARACTER CAUSES A SCENE TO BE SEEN, THEN WE ARE NOT OF GOD AND WE DON'T KNOW HIM AND HE IS NOT OF US.

-you are the total package-

Earlier, when we mentioned how God said, **"Let us make man in our image, after our likeness,"** we pointed out that there was emphasis put on mankind being made in God's image, with His authority and wisdom attributes instilled first; then the likeness of God's fruitful acts of love, joy, peace, longsuffering, gentleness, goodness, faith, meekness and temperance were produced in mankind second, for an identical identification. Recall the revelation of God's image being superior to His likeness of character. God's image of being a Holy Sovereign God helps us to understand His authority and ours, and how our image must work hand-in-hand with our likeness. We also recognize, God's likeness is what sets our understanding of knowing Him personally apart from knowing Him authoritatively. Likewise, our image of commanding authority is superior to our power of likeness in character. Thankfully, even with Himself, God will never allow the powers of His likeable character to ever have control over or supersede the authority of His image; nor will He ever allow the commanding authority of His image have control over or supersede the powers of His likeness. Could you imagine, God without one or the other in either scenario? If you think we're out of control, think again. We are truly grateful. **TO GOD BE THE GLORY!** Remember, like God, we too will have to always have a checks and balances system in place to maintain a healthy control of power in image with our powers in likeness in our lives.

your image of authority is stolen

So how are we connecting the dots as it pertains to mankind? What this is saying is, at minimum man should have a checks and balances system in place too. A checks and balances system in place to maintain order, a healthy control of power in image along with maintaining a balanced order over our powers of character in our own likenesses. We are going to give God all the glory for all of His creations, including us. Just think, He has a checks and balances system in place even within Himself. When He created mankind, we automatically were made the same, but sadly our check for control of power in our image has been compromised and unchecked for quite some time. And an unchecked image leaves an imbalance in our powers of likeness; and so, there is lack in healthy control of authority. Simply put, we lost our image of authority and there is no control; and when there is no control, there is no true power. When Adam and Eve sinned against God, we all lost the absolute component of His image in authority, which makes us who we are, the component we don't understand, and yet still seem to abuse and object to. We all lost our true image of power in authority. When we have the proper understanding of our image to possess the power of authority we are supposed to have, then we have the ability to balance the powers of our likeness. And since we gave up the image powering our authority, we make it easy for our life in flesh to contend with our life in spirit. "***For the flesh lusteth against the Spirit, and the Spirit against the flesh: and these are contrary the one to the other: so that ye cannot do the things ye would.***"(Galatians 5:17)

What we fail to recognize is the truth of the matter. The truth of the matter is we don't like control, which clearly explains why we lack self-control. And for this reason, we have a hard time with understanding God's character when the time comes for Him to exercise His authority to maintain the control we need. We don't recognize the truth in what God's control is; and we don't understand when God uses His power in it, thereof.

Overall, mankind has clearly lived a life of misunderstanding, from what it lacks; but we must admit, Jehovah Jireh has definitely provided some true manna from Heaven in this book for us during these end times. If we don't remember anything else from this book, what we need to remember and lock into our understanding is this, Satan stole the power of our image in authority that killed the life of our spirit, which is destroying our character of likeness. We also must remember, when He sinned against God, he lost his power too. But the difference is we have the favor of God through His covenant with Abraham and Satan doesn't.

HALLELUJAH, THANK YOU JESUS!

All-in-all, you are the total package. We are the total package of God. God, the Holy Spirit consists of the total power of image and likeness. Hence, God has the true balance of power, and so the total power of the Holy Spirit goes like this:

IMAGE
Authority and Wisdom

LIKENESS
Love, Peace, Joy, Longsuffering, Gentleness, Goodness, Faith, Meekness, and Temperance.

We call this the total power of the Holy Spirit! And so, as long as we believe, receive, and accept Jesus, we have the total package of power too!

Diagram 4

THE TOTAL POWER OF THE HOLY SPIRIT

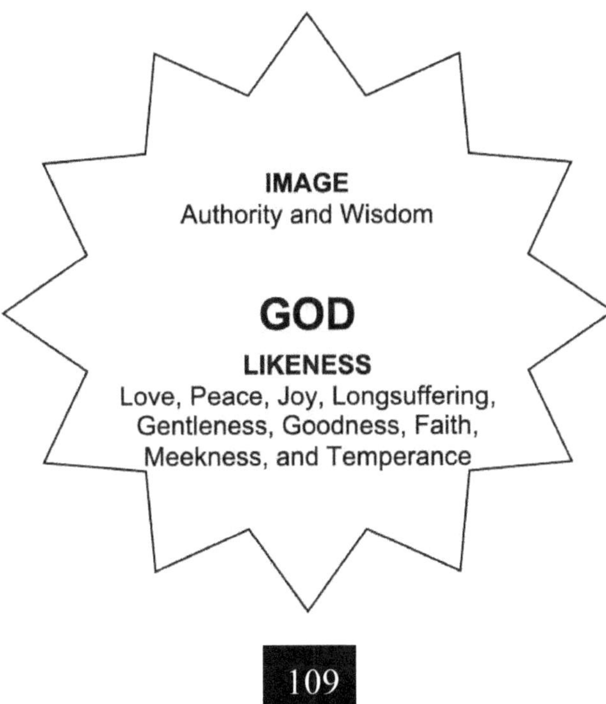

In summary, The Body of God is God the Father, God the Son, and God the Holy Spirit; and the powerful essence of The Body of God comprises of God's Image of Power in Authority and Wisdom; and God's Likeness of Power in Character consisting of Love, Peace, Joy, Longsuffering, Gentleness, Goodness, Faith, Meekness and Temperance. Now, the body of mankind on the other hand has two life forms, a spirit lifeform, from Father God, and a natural lifeform, from Mother Earth. The natural lifeform is meant to work in unison with the spirit lifeform with its primary function being to house the spirit lifeform. And when I say work in unison, I mean these two lifeforms weren't supposed to ever contend with one another; but they were meant to work alongside one another, to manage their other counterparts, the mind, soul, and conscience through a healthy life cycle. The cool thing is, they both can see, smell, taste, touch and hear, so then why are they fighting? The Bible says, "*For the flesh luseth against the Spirit, and the Spirit against the flesh: and these are contrary to one to the other: so that ye cannot do the things ye would.*"(Galatians 5:17) They are fighting over the power for authority. The spirit lifeform rightfully has the power of authority over the natural lifeform, but the spirit lifeform isn't going to force the issue; because it knows it's right, while the natural lifeform is going to fight until the issue is dead right along with it. "*For They that are after the flesh do mind the things of the flesh; but they that are after the Spirit the things of the Spirit. For to be carnally minded is death; but to be spiritually minded is life and peace.*"(Romans 8:5-6) Knowing this information gives us the opportunity of making a well-informed decision for siding with who we are. Are you going to side with the spirit lifeform or the natural lifeform? In the end, you are better off choosing the side God made for us as mankind and be grateful that you are the total package.

-who are you?-

You are the total package. You just have to claim it. You are created as spirit, formed a man in the image and likeness of Almighty God with the power you have from God reclaimed through Christ Jesus. "**He that hath the son hath life; and he that hath not the Son of God hath not life.**"**(1 John 5:12)** In Book One, Chapter 1 Who Are You, of this book series, you have regained an understanding of your total true identity. There is no half stepping. You Are Living Truth! "**For the truth's sake, which dwelleth in us, and shall be with us for ever.**"**(2 John 1:2)** As we said earlier in this chapter, You Are Living Truth because anything that couldn't be proven as true is otherwise false. Living Truth is something that is true proven by its existence. You are still reading this book right now proves you still exist, so you are living truth; and your existence is proof this statement is true. Again, when we prove existence because of its existence, then we prove there is a life source of existence. "**Now Faith is the substance of things hoped for, the evidence of things not seen.**"**(Hebrews 11:1)** THE TRUTH is the evidence as we know Him is God, and anything created by God in His glorious fruit of faith is the substance that was hoped for that either exists, or is living to talk about it, is Living Truth. And yup, this book is living truth, as its existence was inspired by THE TRUTH to give you life. As "**all things were made by him; and without him was not** *any thing made that was made."***(John 1:3)** You Are Living Truth. You are the Living Truth who now needs to determine are you living truth in the existence of walking dead as You #1; or are you living truth living to talk about it, living in the truth as You #2.

Who Are You? You are God's masterpiece. You are the masterpiece of God's original creation, unfortunately walking in a malfunctioned formation. Now, God's intentions for man's kind are for man to live on the earth as You #2's. Originally, we were supposed live as You #1's. Man's original place in the chain for its way of life was #1 and in God's eyes we are #1, so it's a good thing God had a backup plan, a plan B for His You #2's. Yes, we get to do it again. "***And so it is written, The First man Adam was made a living soul; the last Adam was made a quickening spirit.***"**(1 Corinthians 15:45) IT'S TIME FOR REVIVAL, IT'S TIME FOR SOME RESURRECTING POWER TO COME UPON GOD'S PEOPLE, IT'S TIME FOR SOME ACTION; BECAUSE GOD IS MOVING! ARE YOU READY? WHO ARE YOU? ONLY KNOWING WHO YOU ARE WILL DETERMINE IF YOU ARE.**

are you, you #1?
Who are you? Are you, You #1, an existing soul, walking aimlessly about the earth with no life and truth within you? Unfortunately, You #1's are existing souls walking aimlessly about the earth with no life and truth in them, as You #1's are walking in the defects of sin. You #1's are the portion of the living truth that is made up of the living matter often times wondering if they really matter. This group of living truth

clearly don't know God. They don't understand God. They don't know God's love and they don't feel deserving of His love. They lack the capacity to know and understand God because they are missing the primary being of God, His Spirit. Moreover, they will fail to communicate and won't know how to communicate with Him or plainly misunderstand what our Heavenly Father is saying; because they are not speaking in His language, in the natural language of His creation, love. Therefore, God's love and the power thereof is denied. You #1's are existing souls walking aimlessly about the earth with no life and truth within them, because God isn't abiding within them. They are dependent on and of the things of this world. Their life revolves around this world. They look to this worldly system to give them answers to questions only God can answer. Often times they think they have it all-together or either they don't have it all-together because of their worldly accomplishments. And that's just it, You #1's resides in the world, while You #2's abides in God. You #1's don't know Christ, and they don't know You #2. You #1's are walking in the defects of sin. You #1's are walking in the malfunction of their natural formed selves, lacking the creation of their Father's image of godliness within them. You #1's lacking the creation of their Father's image of godliness leaves them powerless, there is no authority and there is no wisdom, they are simply walking aimlessly on the earth. There is no aim, no target, no clear direction to where they are going. While there is no form or power of godliness within You #1's, there is also an imbalance, a malfunction with their Father's creation of likeness. Yup, their fruits are all off. Some have even gone bananas. I'm really laughing out loud right now,

I just had to get that out there. In all honesty, they just don't have the Father's character, no matter how hard they try. And anytime you want to know something about someone, all you have to do is look to their character. You will automatically know whether or not they carry the fruit of God the Father. You will be able to discern whether they are operating in You #1 or functioning in You #2.

My prayer is that this message is infiltrating a desire for You #1's to walk in the promise of their You #2. And if this helps you, I admit, it was an adjustment for me to walk away from my You #1 too. By God's grace, I'm now walking in my You #2, and getting used to my new wineskin. Since I was introduced to my You #2, my life is so much easier. You truly must wholeheartedly surrender. When you do, living in the truth is so easy, it's effortless. It's like plopping on your bed and trusting that your bed is going to support you without letting you fall. The irony of it all is we will trust our beds before we trust God. And just like that bed, God wants you to totally surrender to Him too. He wants you to transfer everything that you have ever entrusted the devil to do for you over to Him. I don't think we even realize that living in the devil's lies is so much harder. I mean, you can literally pick up pain and problems in bulk at the bulk store. Listen, when you are in agreement to walk into the life of your You #2, all you have to do is live your life 'as it is written' for you according to God's purpose and plans for you. It's just that simple. Are you in that place in your life right now, where you are looking for "*Calgon*" to take you away? Are you in that place right now where you are pliable enough, cracked enough or even just enough for God to pour His mercy out on you, to show you The Book He Has Written, 'as it is written' for you? If you are in that place, step out on faith, meet your Creator, claim your You #2 owner's manual, allow God to be God in your life, and allow Him to do the necessary work to give you an abundant life. You must decide. The choice is yours. Currently, **YOU ARE NOT LIVING IN THE TRUTH**, the life as you know it now will only be the introduction to the life you are about to LIVE.

are you, you #2?
Who are you? Are you, You #2, are you a living spirit living in your truth? Have you taken that necessary step of introducing the blueprints of your You #1 to your You #2. We all have to start from somewhere. It's the only way we allow for God to take us from where we are, to where He wants us to be. Where has He taken you from, using the boiler plate of yourself for the greater good? If you are walking in your You #2, Congratulations! This most certainly is a blessing and a milestone all at the same time. You #2's are living truth living in the truth. You #2's have the redemption of Jesus Christ. You #2's only rely on the direction of their Heavenly Father's voice in everything they do. You #2's have surrendered their life over to Father God and allowed Him to take the lead in their life. You #2's are living the wonderful promises of God. I could say that You #2's are living their best life, but that would be an understatement, when in fact they are living their blessed life. The favor of God is on their life. You truly become living proof of living truth when you start living in the truth, then begin to tell others about it. You start living in the truth that you were meant to live. Your ability to live and begin to tell others

about it is your testimony, it is your testimony of the good news for others who are existing. It is your testimony of good news to share with other fellow brothers and sisters you will come to fellowship with. You #2's are the Living Truth that is living proof God does exist. When you are living in the truth, you are in alignment with God's plans for your life. You are in God's will for your life. You are in your Father's Will. It's nice to know when you have been left in a relative's will, but to know that you are walking in the inheritance of your Heavenly Father's perfect will for your life is greater than any inheritance left for you in any man's will on Earth. I mean take your pick, last will and testament, for the gold, or God's Will and Testament, for God's glory.

You #2's are the living truth living in the truth of the total package. You #2's are growing towards living in the capacity of their image of godly authority and wisdom; and their likable character of love, joy, peace, longsuffering, gentleness, goodness, faith, meekness, and temperance, in which there are no laws against these spirits. And when God's Spirit resides in the temple of You #2's, He expects to live like a King "***Thus saith the Lord, The heaven is my throne, and the earth is my footstool: where is the house that ye build unto me? and where is the place of my rest?***"**(Isaiah 66:1)** WHEN **YOU ARE LIVING IN THE TRUTH**, YOU ARE THE LIVING TEMPLE OF GOD. "***What? know ye not that your body is the temple of the Holy Ghost which is in you, which ye have of God, and ye are not of your own? For ye are bought with a price: therefore glorify God in your body, and in your spirit, which are God's.***"**(1 Corinthians 6:19-20)** You #2's, the life as you know it now will be the introduction to the ongoing manifestation of God's love that will take you from glory to glory to glory to glory.

conclusion

Was Chapter 1 a mouth full or what? It was quite the awakening to the introduction of a lifetime, huh? For centuries, man has led themselves to think they could continue in existence only skin deep. WELL, BEHOLD GOD IS DOING A NEW THING! If you haven't read the Bible but may HAVE HEARD THE STORIES RELEVANT TO THE SEASON WE ARE IN, you better LISTEN UP AND LISTEN UP WELL. GOD IS DOING A NEW THING AND YOU DON'T WANT TO MISS IT! This book has a part in what God is doing. For starters, God sure showed up and showed out with some pretty solid answers for telling us WHO WE ARE. He went above and beyond the earthly realm for telling us who we are. Since mankind spent the time and effort to seek their natural lineage, God stepped in to provide man necessary truth about their spiritual heritage. And according to God's ways, you will especially want to heed this warning, if you are living in your You #1. God knows the path you are going down, especially if He knows what He has written for you. The lie you are living is not the truth He has written for you. The truth the enemy is distorting, to steal from you, to have you live a life of lies consisting of hurt, struggle and pain. You #1, God is seeking you. He is gifting You the opportunity to claim the victory that has already been won through Christ Jesus, to take your inheritance back to living the life of who you truly are. You #1, you are the 1 who is literally experiencing your awakening to the introduction of a lifetime. If anyone still has questions on whether God is good or not, well here's your answer. GOD IS GOOD! And now for you You #2's, God is encouraging you. He is gifting You the opportunity to maintain the claim to the victory, to stay on course with what He has already written for you. Whether you are on course, fell off a little, and need to do an about face, or just simply need to come to higher grounds in what He has written, or rewritten for your promotion; you have the right to make stakes in your claim and bind any devils in the process of getting in the way of your destiny. Jesus suffered for us all, and now God is conducting a wakeup call. Even though our **_genealogy_** is already spelled out for us in the **Book of Genesis**, God does it again. Genesis already answers the questions about our **_GENES_**, which was inspired by the breath of God to give us the answers to life to begin with. "***All scripture is given by inspiration of God, and is profitable for doctrine, for reproof, for correction, for instruction in righteousness: That the man of God may be perfect, thoroughly furnished unto all good works.***"*(2 Timothy 3)*

Now, that you have been **REVIVED** with this new breath of life from our Heavenly Father, what are you going to do with this information? Your life as you recognize it today, what are you going to do? My recommendation would be to go through each section of this chapter again, honestly identify and document where you feel you are today, so at least you will have a starting point on how to proceed for tomorrow. "***For his anger endureth but a moment; in his favour is life: weeping may endure for a night, but joy cometh in the morning.***"**(Psalm 30:5)** You can reach a true believer in Christ at iamthe1ministries.org for assistance with helping you to begin your journey. God has equipped us to help you grow toward your next steps, so don't worry, you do have a support system.

Look how hip our Dad is. He literally set this book up according to how we naturally recognize birthdays today, by chapter. Well guess what, no matter where you are in your life today, this is your Chapter 1. Today is your first spiritual birthday. Knowing WHO YOU ARE is Chapter 1 of your spiritual birth, to start a new beginning with your Father God in Heaven, in Jesus' name. Amen. ***HAPPY BIRTHDAY!***

**"The part where the second Adam tells
the first Adam to breath."** -Katina Rodgers-

When your mixed emotions and celebrations are done, collect your thoughts, because the ride is about to get bumpy. You are about to get a whole lot more understanding on WHERE YOU ARE FROM, in Chapter 2, the next chapter of your life. See you in Book 2 & Workbook 2 of this series!

TAKING NOTES

GLOSSARY

¹Abide- remain, last or reside.

¹Acting- conduct oneself.

¹Author- creator.

²*Body of God*- one body operating in the three parts of God, which made up of God, the Father, God, the Son, and God, the Holy Spirit conducting their respective functions within their body as God.

²*Blueprints*- to produce a duplicate of an original.

¹Character- trait or distinctive combination of traits.

²*Checks and Balances*- a restraint in place to counteract a force or an influence for maintaining equilibrium.

¹Created- bring into being.

¹Emotions- intense feeling.

¹Faith- belief and trust in God.

¹Feel- seem.

¹Formed- shape, mold, give form or shape to.

²*Fruit*- the seed of one's essence, the identifier of character, a trait.

¹Genes- segment of DNA that controls inheritance of a trait.

¹Genealogy- study of family pedigrees.

[2]**His purpose**- the outcome of God's intended aim, intention; the results for resolution.

[1]**Idol**- image of a god, object of devotion.

[2]**Idolatry**- a man-made image, concept or object; the practice of worshipping/giving more attention to a man-made image, concept or object; worshipping a man-made concept of a god; creating a false image of; devotion to a false concept; devotion to an object; devotion given to an image, object, or a concept more than that is given to the true and living God; man-made gods which becomes the center of man's attention.

[2]**Imprinted**- engraved, an engraving of ideas or details.

[1]**Lights**- radiation that makes vision possible; source of light; public knowledge;

[1]**Plans**- method for accomplishing something.

[1]**Power**- position of authority; physical might; force or energy used to work.

[1]**Product**- something produced.

[1]**Manifest**- make evident.

[2]**Real Author**- authentic, true creator.

[2]**Sweet**- kind, rewarding, loveable, and pleasant.

RESOURCES

This book is based off the sound doctrine of the King James Version of the Holy Bible. As references were taken from the following sites hosting the King James Version.

bibleref.com

biblegateway.com

blueletterbible.com

webstersdictionary1828.com

https://www.allabouttruth.org/how-many-people-wrote-the-bible-faq.htm

https://www.josh.org/resources/spiritual-growth/attributes-of-god/?mwm_id=315706997961&mot=J79GNF&gclid=Cj0KCQiA2ZCOBhDiARIsAMRfv9LNgCX_CRaWVRt1y_0PkEgbyIQ83wxD6yjtnjQrTwq42neFCCkv4G0aAu3zEALw_wcB

The Perfect Wave. Directed by Bruce Macdonald, performances by Scott Eastwood, Cheryl Ladd and Patric Lyster, 2014.

[1]Webster's Dictionary Of The English Language Created In Cooperation With The Editors of Merriam-Webster, 2014, Federal Street Press

[2]Italicized definitions were created by Katina Rodgers in conjunction with the Holy Spirit, 2022, I Am The 1 Ministries

ABOUT THE AUTHOR

Scan the QR Code below to discover how I experienced my awakening to the introduction of a lifetime. You will learn how God took the good, bad and the ugly from my You #1 and cultivated it for His purpose and the greater good of my You #2. Continue to journey with me to understand what it takes to maintain living in the truth of You #2.

This book was written by Katina Rodgers for
I Am The 1 Ministries Spirit School
Join I Am The 1 Ministries Spirit School to
train not to be conformed by your You #1,
but to be transformed by your You #2.
Get more information at iamthe1ministries.org

TAKE YOUR STEPS TO SALVATION TODAY!

*"I say to you that likewise there will be more joy in heaven over one sinner who repents than over ninety-nine just persons who need no repentance."***(Luke 15:7)**

ARE YOU THE 1? Claim your inheritance of God's Promise to you. When you claim your right as a child of God, you will receive God's free gift of salvation. FOLLOW THESE SIMPLE STEPS TO SALVATION AND YOU WILL BE SAVED. THE TIME IS NOW!

ADMIT *you are a sinner*
ASK GOD *for forgiveness*
BELIEVE GOD *sent HIS only begotten SON to die for our sins*
RECEIVE JESUS' *free gift of salvation*
ACCEPT JESUS *as LORD AND SAVIOR over your life*
AGREE *with God's promises for your life*

YOU ARE THE 1
YOU ARE THE CHURCH, AND
THE CHURCH IS IN YOU!

GOD WANTS TO HEAR FROM YOU, start your personal relationship with Jesus today! HE WILL ACCEPT YOU AS YOU ARE. All you have to do is start talking to HIM. If you are unsure of what to say, start with the Lord's prayer.

Our Father which art in heaven, Hallowed by thy name. Thy kingdom come, Thy will be done in earth, as it is in heaven. Give us this day our daily bread. And forgive us our debts, as we forgive our debtors. And lead us not into temptation, but deliver us from evil: For thine is the kingdom, and the power, and the glory, for ever. Amen. Matthew 6:9-13

www.ingramcontent.com/pod-product-compliance
Lightning Source LLC
Chambersburg PA
CBHW071444130726
47997CB00006B/2222